M000188750

Awaken
to
ℐUnconditional
Love

Awaken
to
Unconditional
Love

NEW WISDOM FROM
20 SPIRITUAL MASTERS

Don Fedor, PhD

O'LEARY
PUBLISHING
The Influencer's Press

BONITA SPRINGS, FL

Copyright © 2021 by Don Fedor

All rights reserved.

Published in the United States by
O'Leary Publishing
www.olearypublishing.com

The views, information, or opinions expressed in this book
are solely those of the authors involved and do not necessarily
represent those of O'Leary Publishing, LLC.

ISBN: 978-1-952491-09-2 (print)
ISBN: 978-1-952491-10-8 (ebook)
Cataloging-in-Publication Data is on file with the Library of Congress.

Editing by Heather Davis Desrocher
Proofreading by S.R. Boland and Sharman Monroe
Illustrations by Jonathan Rambinintsoa
Cover and interior design by Jessica Angerstein

Printed in the United States of America

A portion of the proceeds from this book will be donated to charity.

To All of My Teachers
Known & Unknown

Love requires nothing to change; yet
It allows everything to change.

— from Moses's Message

Contents

Preface

"Why are we here?" How many of us have wrestled with this soul-searching question? It seems regardless of the number of times this question has been posed, and regardless of the countless answers offered, we still wonder about our purpose here on earth. This quest has birthed religions, spiritual perspectives, and philosophies throughout the world. In many ways, this question has challenged and perplexed us since the dawn of human consciousness.

What if our true purpose in life, our reason for being here, is to learn to embody Unconditional Love? What if all of life's challenges, and experiences, are really opportunities to live from the deep love within us, and thus awaken to our authentic selves? Unconditional Love just might allow everything to change without actually requiring anything to be different.

Does this resonate with you? Check in with your higher self and see if this is your truth. Could your purpose, and mine, be to learn how to embody Unconditional Love? What would our lives look like if only Love remained?

For many years, I've reflected on what it would mean to live from a place of Unconditional Love amidst our ever-changing world. We seem to be in a particularly chaotic period, with global health challenges, divisive political currents, continuing environmental degradation, and the surfacing of deep-seated societal questions around human rights and justice.

How would our feelings, thoughts, and responses be different if our natural view of the world was one of Unconditional Love? I sensed its all-encompassing potential, but getting a handle on such an abstract concept seemed impossible. It didn't make any sense for me to chase such an ideal that has eluded so many.

Yet, as much as I tried, I couldn't shake this fundamental question. I knew on an intuitive level that my understanding of Unconditional Love paled in comparison to its magnificent truth. Even if I could come to know the length and breadth of such love, how could I awaken Unconditional Love in my own life, and how might it help others? It seemed there were far more questions than answers.

I knew the old Biblical saying, "Ask, and it will be given to you; seek, and you will find." So, based on a flash of insight, I decided to ask, via an energy connection, a group of Masters from diverse spiritual and religious traditions for their help. This book is the result of what they had to say. It is an immersion into Unconditional Love — the true essence of ourselves — guided by a group of twenty Masters including Jesus, Buddha, Athena, Moses, and Krishna.

Introduction

Many spiritual traditions hold Unconditional Love as the ultimate state of being to attain. It is known by different names: *a state of grace, nirvana,* or *enlightenment.* It is a common theme in many spiritual philosophies. So why isn't Unconditional Love discussed more frequently? I believe it is because Unconditional Love feels completely unattainable or extremely impractical in our busy lives, thus better left to saints, gods, or angelic beings.

I encountered a hesitance for many of us to discuss the topic of Unconditional Love at a friend's Christmas party some years ago. Having recently retired from Georgia Tech in Atlanta, where I was a professor of Organizational Behavior, I found it difficult to answer the question, "What are you up to these days?" When I reluctantly admitted that I was writing a book on Unconditional Love, this often brought the conversation to an abrupt halt. Aside from the occasional, "Oh that's nice," people didn't know what to say about such a lofty pursuit. The most surprising part of the evening was that amongst those with a befuddled response were a priest and a professor of religion. I sensed that, even for them, this was an uncomfortable topic.

Another reason this topic may be difficult is that most of us don't have a feel for Unconditional Love. While we really want to believe that it is possible, many of us grew up in religions where we needed to earn God's love. There were numerous things we had to do — like asking for forgiveness for our sins, or doing penance — to earn God's blessings. We seem to have difficulty with the idea of being loved unconditionally, and even more trouble believing that Unconditional Love resides within us as a seed we can cultivate.

My hope in creating this book is to help you experience a new awakening to Unconditional Love. This is not about love in relationships with a special person — there are countless books on this topic. This is not about love based on sacrifice or subjugation of the self — there are probably too many books written from this perspective as well. This book is about the state of Being wherein we discover our truest nature, where we live in peace, acceptance, gratitude, and joy. It is about following the deep yearnings of the divine love that created us. Such love transcends our material success, the enjoyment of our avocations, whether or not we have a partner, or the value of our possessions.

While this description can strike a positive note in us, it can also sound like another set of new-age ideals: lofty and impractical. It sounded so for me as well, until the Masters brought new aspects of Unconditional Love alive.

What does the embodiment of Unconditional Love mean for those of us who don't consider ourselves saints or sages? I believe it means freedom from much of the suffering we endure at our own hands. It releases us from the bondage of the ego (the part of us that believes we are finite and that searches for love in all the wrong places). It opens the door to discovering who we truly are.

The Masters

In this book, the nature and wonder of Unconditional Love unfold from the perspectives of twenty Masters. Some of them walked this earth, while others represent ideals to which we aspire. All of them were selected intentionally, based upon what I sensed was their desire to speak to us about Unconditional Love. Each of them brings their own unique viewpoint. Even when these Masters address similar topics, they provide a unique perspective to help us more fully understand, and feel, the qualities of Unconditional Love.

The Masters come from a diverse set of spiritual and religious traditions, and from different times in history. In order to bring their perspectives of Unconditional Love to life, I initially used the form of channeling employed by Neale Donald Walsch (*Conversations with God*). This is sometimes described as automatic writing. In a meditative state, I connected with the energy of each Master and wrote what came to me through that connection.

The Book's Unfolding

As the conduit for this book, I did my best to share the energy of the selected Masters to help with our journey into Unconditional Love. I acknowledge that anyone who channels will affect the messages received, no matter who they are or how well they channel. The translator will always influence the translation, and I am certainly no exception. I hope that, while the words are mine, the essence of what was recorded is true to each Master.

I am grateful for the messages the Masters shared with me, as there were many wonderful surprises in what they had to say. Working with them dramatically changed my life (more about this in the Highlights, Themes, and Personal Note sections).

You might be wondering why someone who believes in a singular God, or Creator of All That Is, channeled all of these different Masters. My answer is that I felt divinely inspired to do so. Unconditional Love is not exclusive to any one spiritual path or limited to any particular set of religious practices.

The Bible says that God works in mysterious ways, and through numerous agents (e.g., angelic beings), to help us move "toward the light." I believe that my inspiration to channel these Masters was Source's way of helping me discover the many aspects of Unconditional Love, which I had never consciously considered.

My initial notes from the Masters were rough and often looked more like hastily-scribbled outlines than intelligible prose. As a result, what emerged from those early writings has gone through numerous rewrites to smooth them out and make them more understandable. With each revision, I did my best to be guided by that Master.

With help from a dear friend, we grouped their messages along three general experiences (this turned out to be more of a challenge than anticipated), focusing on whether the Master's message was primarily about:

1. Going Within,
2. Rising Above, or
3. Living in the Light.

In Part I, *Going Within*, the Masters address the need for us to shift our focus from what is outside ourselves, to what resides within — the Unconditional Love that is our essential nature. This message comes from Siddhartha Gautama (the Buddha), St. Francis, Athena, Thoth, Jesus, Aengus, and Paramahansa Yogananda.

In Part II, *Rising Above*, Krishna, Babaji, Maitreya, White Tara, Parvati, Ganesh, and Quan Yin speak about rising above our daily experiences so that we may live in the essences of joy, gratitude, and forgiveness.

In Part III, *Living in the Light*, Archangel Michael, Amaterasu, Mother Mary, Moses, Saint-Germain, and Mother Earth guide us to step out of our self-imposed shadows and shine our light.

In Parts IV and V, the themes and ideas that emerged from the entire group of Masters are explored, and how we might better understand and embody this love.

Part IV, *Unearthed Themes*, begins with the nature of Unconditional Love and then explores the themes of relationships, judgment, responsibility, emotions, sacrifice, forgiveness, vulnerability, life's distractions, and our motivation to change — as they run through the Masters' messages.

Part V, *Conclusions*, explores why Unconditional Love is so important, how we can experience it, and our individual contributions to it.

Living Unconditional Love is a journey that has been at our core since the dawn of time. It would be wonderful if, with the help of the Masters, it became a more integral part of our lives, and allowed us to see beyond the illusions of our differences.

Given that this book is for my benefit as well as others, in the *Personal Note* section, I offer how this journey with the Masters has transformed my life.

Your Journey With the Masters

It will be quickly evident that this book is not a novel to be read from front to back. Instead, it is meant to be enjoyed over and over again as you converse with the Masters on multiple levels.

Depending on where you are now, you will experience Unconditional Love from your own unique perspective. The Masters with whom you resonate may be different from those who speak to another and may evolve as you continue to grow in your knowledge and understanding of Unconditional Love. Let us begin the journey of discovering which Masters open doors to new insights and perspectives for you. They all lovingly await you.

Part I
Going Within

Knowing Our True Selves

Guidance for Reading the Messages in Part I

In the following messages, the Masters address the need for us to shift our focus from what is outside ourselves to what resides within — the Unconditional Love that is our essential nature.

To know our true selves, we must see through the illusions and false identities that we have taken on and release them. The Masters in this section discuss all that is NOT us, and all that distracts us from knowing our authentic self. They remind us that the things of this world are often a distraction. Finally, they explore the essence of our true selves.

As you read this section, it may be helpful to keep the following questions in mind:

What can I do to eliminate non-essential distractions?

What keeps me focused on the world of external events?

Where do I want to place my attention and focus?

The Buddha

Siddhartha
Gautama

The Buddha

Nepal

563 – 483 BC

Advocate of the Middle Path

Siddhartha, who became The Buddha, teaches that moderation is the way to pursue a spiritual life. For a period in his life, following his departure from the luxuries of being a king's son, he tried severe austerity and deprivation. He had witnessed the suffering in the world and immersed himself in it with the hope of spiritual awakening. Yet, he made no progress. He eventually had an epiphany that such extreme practices were pointless.

As a result, Siddhartha taught that although life is full of suffering, caused by craving and desire, we can eliminate suffering by withdrawing our attention from the chaos of the world, and by leading a moral, mindful, and compassionate life. He asserted that by living a moderate life, or following "the middle way," we achieve happiness and peace.

Buddha can help us when we feel a yearning in our souls for that which is beyond our physical selves — when we desire to know the truth of our essence.

Your True Essence

The Buddha's Message

I call to all who now seek enlightenment. I am the Buddha and I come to you as I have throughout the ages to help you find that pathway to yourself. While the world has changed much since I appeared to you in human form, over 2,500 years ago, my message to you remains the same.

To uncover the Unconditional Love of the true self requires transcending the chaos in which you find yourself. The material world calls for your constant attention from the moment you open your eyes to each new day. Among your mobile devices, televisions, workplaces, road systems, and personal lives, there is no end to the information and chaotic energy bombarding you in every moment. This chaos even invades the quietude of your slumber. This is why so many of you cannot settle down to sleep at night.

Hear me when I tell you that the human, material world and your true nature do not coexist well. Your essence, and the wellspring from which it emanates, is found in the quietude of meditation. Retreat from all that is around you to find out who and what you are.

Be not surprised if you find this difficult to do. Many have become addicted to constant stimulation, and their bodies are dependent on the associated adrenaline. The mind wants to constantly race from issue to issue, and problem to problem. The mind knows its job and does it well, but does not know you, or your true essence, and no amount of thinking can change this.

I call upon you to be as dedicated to discovering yourself, and your connection to the Divine, as you have been to earthly success. Create time and space in your life for this to happen. It will not occur if you don't allow for it. Relentlessly chasing an identity based on what the world defines as important will not lead you to the peace and love that is your very core.

The portal for this journey is meditation focused on the energy of your spiritual heart. Your heart is your connection to the Divine, and all that is in creation. It might seem that spending time focused on yourself is wrong when there is so much to be done.

Nothing could be further from the truth. Many of the things that you now feel are so critical will fade away — just like the great cities of old have turned to dust, and entire societies have passed out of humanity's memory. Even massive continents have disappeared below the sea. Everything of the earth is destined to give up its physical form. What does endure forever is your very essence. It will last throughout time, and beyond, and is that which now calls to you. It is the YOU that will not only transform your own life, but all of those lifetimes throughout time. The cycle of lifetime after lifetime of solely attending to earthly concerns is coming to an end. Bring forth the love in your heart, and be the transformation for which you have so longed.

What I cannot tell you is what form of meditation to use. Nor do I advocate any particular method. Through the ages, there have been countless techniques offered as the *one way* to meditate. Yet regardless of how they are taught, your experience of them will always be unique. Try different methods and see what resonates with you. One is no better than another. The one or ones for you will lead you to self-discovery, and your own true heartbeat.

I caution you to not be rigid in your meditation practices. Follow your intuition, curiosity, and your guides. They will lead you to other forms of meditation that will open new vistas of love and peace for you. I would be honored to be one of your guides. I only await your invitation to join you on your spiritual journey.

Make space and time for yourself. Ease your overactive mind and slip into the essence of yourself. This journey will reward you beyond measure.

I sit believing all things are possible, and so will you.

Reflection

Resting in the Peace of Your Essence

Imagine the Buddha, the teacher of mindfulness and compassion, here with you. Feel his energy. Connect with him in whatever way feels most comfortable to you, such as in meditation, or by seeking silence.

Ask him the following questions, and absorb his answers...

Why am I attracted to the constant stimulation?

What can I let go of that no longer serves me?

How can I create more space in my life?

How do I connect with my inner essence?

How can I begin to meditate or deepen my current practice?

What message do you have for me?

Do this regularly and see how the answers change.

St. Francis
of Assisi

St. Francis of Assisi

Assisi, Italy

1181 – 1226 AD

Humble Animal Lover

It is interesting that both Siddhartha and St. Francis began life in wealthy homes, but chose to leave those comforts to seek their own truths. Siddhartha chose a journey of moderation, while St. Francis chose to remain on the path of austerity, living a difficult life of fasting and discomfort.

St. Francis wandered as a pilgrim, preaching and tending the ill (especially those with leprosy). While he accomplished many things, his affinity for animals is how most people remember him. He would preach to the birds and other wild animals, and it is reported that they gathered around and were still, attentive, and tame in his presence.

St. Francis passionately shared his love of God with all fellow creatures. His simple message of universal love has always inspired a great following, and to this day, he is one of the most beloved saints. He is credited with introducing the creche to the Christian nativity.

St. Francis stands as a humble example of one who was able to love God's creations regardless of their form (animal or human) or condition (diseased or healthy). What a valuable example for us today in a world that challenges us to respond with love!

Love Is Tender

St. Francis's Message

I bring you greetings from all those who love you and want you to better know the nature of Unconditional Love. What I hope to help you with is the gentleness of love that encompasses all. Much of what you encounter in your world has an edge or sharpness to it. If you stub your toe or make a mistake, there can be painful physical and emotional consequences. When you catch yourself doing something incorrectly, or what you consider to be wrong, you are often hard on yourself.

The love you seek is a love of tenderness and understanding. This is especially true when dealing with yourself. Beating yourself up for what you think you lack, or for what you are, serves no purpose other than to hold you in the same pattern. You are not perfect and were never meant to be. Every person is trying to discover who he or she is. Some will figure it out sooner rather than later, but all are on the same ultimate journey.

Soften your self-criticism and transform it into acceptance and hope. Accept who and where you are, and gently decide what you'd like to change. Unconditional Love is tender as well as honest. It takes away the stick you beat yourself with, while, at the same time, it asks you to honestly look into the mirror of your soul.

Once you have removed the mask of self-deception, you can begin to follow your heart. The ego creates the illusion of what you need, want, or fear, whereas the heart knows no such limitations. When was the last time you quieted yourself and listened just to your own heartbeat? Ask it to begin to speak to you. Many fear what the heart might say. Might it suggest a life course change, a different set of relationships, or a new career? Such possibilities can raise the fear that you are doing something that is not for your highest good.

Is it really better not to know? If you are harsh with yourself — then, yes. If you can be gentle with yourself — then, no. Your heart is not the enemy to be suppressed; it is your friend to be nurtured and honored. This is your connection to all of the Divine. This cannot be done through the mind. You cannot think your way to your truest desire. It is done only through the energy of the heart.

As are all of the Masters, I am here for you. When you venture into self-criticism and condemnation, call to me. When you need a guide to the love in your heart, ask for my assistance. You are wonderful beyond your imagination. Walk with me on the way to yourself.

Reflection

Listening to Your Heart

In the company of Saint Francis, a compassionate monk who is known for his deep love for animals,

Let your mind rest.

Feel the beat of your heart.

Connect to your heart.

Feel the power and love of your heart.

Ask your heart what it has to say.

See your heart as a doorway to the Divine.

Go through the doorway and see where it leads.

Do this short reflection anytime you need to reset.

Athena

Athena

Greece

Greek Goddess of Wisdom

Athena, the Greek goddess of battle, wisdom, and strategy, is the daughter of Zeus, and a primary goddess in the Greek pantheon. She is the patron deity of Athens. The Parthenon (in Athens, Greece) stands as a tribute to her. In Rome, Athena was known as Minerva.

As a Greek goddess, Athena was no stranger to drama and conflict. The Greek gods were famous for their fights and intrigue, and Athena was often called upon to intercede. As a powerful feminine deity, Athena embodies both strength and wisdom, and stands as a powerful feminine model even in modern times.

Athena is also known for her support of heroes who had to face challenges and destruction. As heroes on our own journeys to further our souls' purpose, we can turn to Athena for guidance when we encounter drama and our demons.

The Distraction of Drama

Athena's Message

Dear Ones, I come to you in love from times long past, and from times in your far future. For all the things you have endured during your time on earth, love is the one constant, yet you find it so elusive. I come now to help you understand better how to <u>hold the love that is you</u>.

One of your greatest challenges is all that is taking place in your lives and around you. It is called drama and it can be as addictive as drugs. The frequency is such that it continues to pull you down into baser energy levels, and it is difficult to ignore. It fuels feelings of hopelessness and negativity.

Your conversations, your news, your computers, and your lives are filled with what is happening in the world. Who is being harmed by whom, who has broken the law, what is happening in the lives of your stars, and who is doing what that seems wrong? It is time to take note of how all of this is affecting you, and the illusion that it creates about what is important in your life.

People focus on this drama with rapt attention, moving from one disaster or news event to another; I ask you, to what avail? Does knowing these things and being emotionally involved in them really change anything? Is any of this helping you be the person you want to be, or is it simply contributing to your fear of making a mistake, or of being the next victim?

The truth is that your attention always changes things. Taking sides or deciding who is right, and who is wrong, feeds this drama with your energy and diverts your attention from what is truly important.

When you seek to be Unconditional Love, you shift your focus from world events to knowing your true self. This can be the place you most fear to go. Yet, your world will never be what you desire by trying to fix it. You must "fix" yourself first. The history of humanity is filled with failed attempts to force others to conform to certain moral codes. The world as you know it has made some progress, but you long for so much more, and the time is now for a new wondrous age.

This will require you to detach from the drama in your life, and that of the larger world around you. You cannot get to that quiet place of love and self-acceptance while being steeped in the chaos of the mind. Your mind wants to be active and be in charge of your thoughts and feelings. It has had this exalted position from the time of your birth. It directs you to evaluate, judge, discern and problem-solve — all supposedly important activities to thrive in the material world.

Where does your mind take you when it isn't occupied? Does it find things to work on, to worry about, or things for you to do? Where do your thoughts naturally go? Do they go to quiet gratitude and joy, or to all that is wrong or worrisome in your life? How much do you need the stimulation of the news? Is being quiet uncomfortable? Must you always find things to keep yourself occupied?

The grand illusion of life is that happiness comes from being connected to the outside world of happenings, with good and bad, right and wrong, winners and losers. I now ask that you halt this treadmill of attending to drama, and redirect your attention to what is important even beyond each lifetime.

You are a Divine being and it is time to know yourself as such. Find the You that transcends all earthly events. Tap into the energy at your source that exists beyond time. It is your choice to stay focused on the drama or to look beyond it to what endures.

On your quest for Unconditional Love, you can call upon me to help you slice away today's illusions. My spear and shield are no longer for battle, but for Truth. As events come forward in the world, allow me to cut through their appearance to reveal what you can learn from them. Sometimes you will learn to let them go and attend to them no more. Other times, you may learn to see the subtle messages of hope and joy, or how the greater good is being served.

By observing your reactions to events, you can gauge to what extent you have removed yourself from drama. I give you these questions to help you release the drama in your daily life: Do I need to know about this? Why should I care about this? Do I need, in any way, to be involved in this situation? Is this mine to fix or change? What possible good can emerge from my involvement in this? What happens to my life if I give this my attention?

My love and support are always with you. Join me in knowing Truth.

Reflection

Releasing Drama

Bring to mind something with which you are struggling.

With the help of the Goddess of wisdom and strategy, ask Athena . . .

What is necessary for me to know or do about this situation?

How can I minimize my involvement in this issue, and the impact of this issue on my life and well-being?

Please show me what is the highest good for all in this situation.

Now allow yourself to find the You that *transcends* all of these events.

Tap into the energy of your source that exists beyond time.

Thoth

Thoth

Egypt

Egyptian God of Learning

As a god in ancient Egypt, Thoth was seen as embodying wisdom and knowledge. He was credited with the creation of many of the Egyptian arts and sciences, including writing (hieroglyphics), astronomy, and medicine. In some stories, he created the universe. He was also credited with a vast knowledge of magic. His magic was so powerful it could control both the forces of nature and the gods themselves. This power, in combination with his wisdom and knowledge, is supposedly the reason for his name — "Thoth" means thrice great.

He was known for speaking the truth and being scrupulously fair. Thoth was the one to decide if a deceased pharaoh remained in the underworld or would be permitted to ascend into the upper world with the gods.

Thoth represents our multidimensional selves — the logical and rational (math and science), and the mythical (magic and the afterlife). He can help us integrate these often disparate aspects of ourselves as we endeavor to move forward spiritually.

Releasing Judgments

Thoth's Message

I speak to you from the time when humanity first began to consider its divine essence. These were times when life itself was infused with the mysteries of humanity's place in the universe. Back when you marveled at the travels of the sun, moon, planets, and stars across the sky, you felt your connection to Mother Earth and the cycles of life itself.

When you look upon what has survived through the ages, from those days long ago, you see the structures, but many of the spiritual ideals from that time have faded away. This fading was meant to be so that when the time was right, you could reawaken your connection to the entirety of all that is. That time is now.

For thousands of years, humanity decided to focus elsewhere and, in so doing, has made great advances. It is now your calling to balance that which was, with that which is, so that you may use both to ascend into higher levels of consciousness. In those ancient times, there was the desire to ascend, upon death, into the upper realms to live with the gods. Humans believed that I determined their fate based on their deeds and transgressions.

It is now time to understand that this was never necessary. You have always been your own judge and jury, and it is time to transcend all judgment. Release all of your judgments, of yourself and of others, so that you may all function in the service of love.

You have always been on the path of ascension. The deities you have worshipped, subjugated yourself to, and placed above you, are reflections of what is inside of you. Over countless ages, you have revered many different deities, depending upon your birthplace, culture, and circumstances. You have worshiped in myriad ways and used different rituals to get you where you are at this time.

Your conscious mind has forgotten most of your former religious and spiritual practices, but they are held within your DNA and behavioral patterns. Some of these continue to serve you, but many are now holding you back. Realize that much of what you experienced over those many lifetimes was of subjugation and feeling unworthy in the presence of your gods.

Take from those past times your connection to everything that occurs in heaven and on earth. Take also from those times the wonderment of all creation. Reawaken to the balance of your essential aspects, including your masculine and feminine, your heart and head, and your strength and gentleness. Combine all of these with your sense of your spiritual self so you may know that you need not bow to anyone or anything. You are a creator. Learn to enjoy not only the mysteries of nature and celestial bodies, but also the mysteries of yourself.

I am here to help you remember and reawaken all that you are. I am here to help you shed those things that hold you back from the love and joy that reside in your essence. Reconnect with those times when you have felt the love, the power, the creativity, the joy of your true self. Shed those times of pain, suffering, remorse, guilt, and lack. The trying times have been strongly encoded within you and are difficult to release. The experience of your true self can fade from your memory. The challenge you face is to release your attachments to the trying times, and to know the truth of who you are.

Like you, I have returned in recreated form, and I am here to assist all who want to ascend and transcend. I no longer serve as a judge, for this does not benefit humanity any longer. I am here to reawaken you to the hidden and forgotten parts of yourself, to the love that you are. The afterlife you sought, lifetime after lifetime, is here now and resides within you.

Each night as you gaze at the moon, remember me, and call upon me to help you. Think back to the mysteries that your soul once pondered, and feel the unfolding of your true self. Join me in wonder at all that we have created and experienced. Go forth without fear, for I am with you now and forever.

Reflection

Release and Recall

As the Egyptian god of wisdom and knowledge, Thoth, the creator of the universe, can help us create our own universe. In Thoth's presence, ask him to support you as you repeat each statement until it feels true . . .

I release beliefs and patterns that no longer serve me.

I let go of any judgments I have held about myself.

I let go of judgments I have of others.

I shed pain, suffering, guilt, and remorse.

I recall times of love, creativity, and joy in my true self.

I bring back the mysteries that will open my soul.

I feel gratitude for the spiritual practices that have brought me here.

Use these statements anytime you have something to release.

Jesus

Jesus

Judea, Palestine

3 BCE - 30 AD

Master of Love

Jesus is considered to be the Son of God, and his teachings are the foundation of Christianity. Many of his followers believe that he was the Messiah foretold in the Old Testament. His resurrection confirmed for them that he is divine.

His central themes of hope, love, forgiveness, and compassion strike a chord with many of us, even if we do not consider ourselves Christians. Jesus' well-known Sermon on the Mount encourages us to love everyone, even our enemies.

During his travels, Jesus performed many miracles in the service of his teachings. While there is little in the Bible about how Jesus lived and where he traveled, other accounts of his life suggest that he received training from Gnostics, the Essenes, and in Egypt's mystery schools.

Jesus can represent the universal ideals and our desire for the miraculous.

Choose Courage Over Fear

Jesus's Message

Dear Ones, you seek to know better the ideal of Unconditional Love. My heart opens to you as I try, once again, to help you understand. Truly, my message from many earth-years ago has been greatly misunderstood. Many have perceived my form of Unconditional Love as allowing harm, and as based on the sacrifice of self. This was not my intention.

I do truly love all, and what I did on earth some two thousand years ago was of transcendence, not suffering. Please believe me that Unconditional Love is rooted in honesty as well as allowance. I did allow those around me to be who they were, and to behave as they did. However, it was me, not them, who decided upon my reactions and responses. When I chose to stand trial and be crucified, it was my decision to show the world that life does not stop with one's physical death. Choosing to do this was consistent with my Unconditional Love for all of humanity.

Hear me when I say it was I who decided this was in the highest good for all concerned. It was not forced on me by those in power at the time. Unfortunately, a lot of humanity has interpreted my act of Unconditional Love as me being victimized by those around me. This is because of humanity's fear of being acted upon.

From the vantage point of Unconditional Love, there are no victims. Instead, there are opportunities and choices. It is time to free yourselves from the pain and suffering of being victimized by the very lives you have chosen. Unconditional Love allows you to stand in your incredible power, to choose how you want to conduct your life, and to decide what you want to bring into your realm of experiences.

I've observed people choosing to be hung on crosses, wearing crowns of thorns, walking across hot coals, suppressing their sexuality, and performing all manner of sacrifices to be more Christlike. Do you think my love for you is based on a desire to see you suffer? Does a mother want her children to experience pain and hardship? What part of Unconditional Love would require you to prove yourself to me or anyone?

I did not come to the earth to demonstrate how to suffer, but how to live as the divine being you are. What was primarily recorded about my life were my deeds. You now have the knowingness to look beyond these to the essence of my being. What do you see and feel? What do you sense in me that is also in you? Do you feel acceptance, allowance, connectedness, contentment, and joy? Do you have a knowingness of who you truly are?

I suggest that you come to me directly to know me, and to receive what I have to share with you. The Unconditional Love I came to show you is who you truly are. It can be expressed toward others in whatever way you choose, but it is not about external relationships. It is about being the love that quietly and gently invites others to know their true selves. It isn't about persuading others to change, or telling others what to do.

The Unconditional Love you seek will appear to require great *courage*: the *courage* to go within and to see all that you are; the *courage* to be honest with yourself; the *courage* to refrain from judgment and condemnation; the *courage* to be a loving observer of yourself and others; and the *courage* to change what is no longer consistent with who you are. But is it really *courage* that you need to do all of this? Courage has often been defined as facing adversity and suffering in the process. It need not be so! Who do you really need to struggle with or resist?

Fear is what you struggle with the most: fear of rejection, fear of your own emotions, fear of being different, fear of loss, fear of the unknown, and fear of the uncertainty of change. Acknowledge your fears, appreciate them for how they have served you, and release them.

If you can forgive yourself, forgiving others is easy. If you can love yourself, loving others is easy. If you can appreciate yourself, and all of your many experiences, then appreciating others and what they have chosen to experience is easy.

Come to me, let go of your preconceptions, and I will help you to be the Unconditional Love that is your essence.

Reflection

Healing

Jesus is a model of love, compassion and healing. With His love and guidance, unfold into the following:

I come into your presence to ...

Heal my wounds;

Discover the places where I've held pain;

Release the judgments I have projected onto others;

Relinquish my suffering;

Allow love to fill all of those spaces where darkness has resided;

Step into my true divinity;

Know I am love; and

Embrace my own light.

Use this reflection as often as you need to heal your wounds.

Aengus

Aengus

Ireland

Celtic God of Lovers

Aengus is the Celtic god of romance and soulmate love, and is believed to protect lovers with his power of invisibility and his magical sword. He is the one to call upon for assistance in finding great love, or to receive help when difficulties arise between lovers.

The story goes that to find his true love, Aengus had to go to a lake where his mate would be among a large group of girls, all of whom were disguised as swans. He had to identify her among the swans, and then she would have the option to choose him. Aengus arrived at the lake and saw the swans serenely swimming in the water. He called to her and she came to him, whereupon he magically changed himself into a swan and they flew away together.

This romantic Celtic god calls to the part of us that longs for inspired love. He, like us, faced the challenges of identifying and attracting his true partner with whom he could soar. Aengus guides us as we prepare and search for our Love, or as we strengthen our intimate relationship.

A Return to Wholeness

Aengus's Message

I am the energies of the twin flame and of hope. Many feel my influence when they long for their true partner. My essence is the merging of our deepest desires to create wholeness. It is the reconnection of the split that occurred when you came into being.

What can I tell you about Unconditional Love? It is the state that you are reawakening to, and it is the answer to your question of returning to wholeness. Most of you feel incomplete even in close relationships. You have looked outside yourselves to try to feel whole. You've had different partners, life interests, addictions, and obsessions, all in the pursuit of completeness. Ultimately, none of these have worked. Intimate relationships lose their passion. Addictions and obsessions lose their luster.

You will never be completed by outside influences, no matter how wonderful or alluring. They cannot do for you what you must do and be for yourself. Much of your energies are divided between your masculine (the doer) and feminine (the feeler) dimensions — the Yin and the Yang.

For you to know true Unconditional Love, there needs to be an integration of these essential energies of the masculine and the feminine. A house divided cannot know the fullness of love; yet you fervently hope that your internal strife will melt away in the presence of affection and attention from another.

Some of the world's religions have understood this truth that Unconditional Love is a state of internal being, and not found in external relationships. What they have misunderstood is that this does not translate into subjugation or self-denial.

Everyone holds within themselves an entire array of beliefs, feelings, and emotions. These all exert their unique influences and are not always consistent or compatible. Because you strive to favor those you believe to be positive, and work to suppress the rest, you often live with internal conflict. Your world is set on fighting all that displeases it, and this is how you then function inside of yourself. This includes trying to combat your fears, unwanted feelings, and unacceptable impulses.

How would it be to love and appreciate those things within you that you have disliked? They have all served a purpose.

In past times, and in other places, they may have been your only way to survive. But now you no longer need them.

The love you seek can only come about through the integration of all the wonderful, sometimes disparate, facets that make you a unique being. Appreciate them all, love them all, and release those that no longer serve your highest good. As longtime residents of your identity, they will not simply fade gently away. These patterns and habits tend to resist our initial efforts. Thank them for coming forward each time they appear, appreciate their contribution, and decide what would now be compatible with who you are – a being of love.

All of what I say may seem strange. Realize, I am offering a joyful marriage of all those conflicting aspects that reside within you. Joyful unions are created through desire and choice, not fear or force. In your society, you have the notion of a shotgun wedding where the bride and groom are married under duress. The chances of such unions leading to anything but hardship is not good. How much of your energy is consumed, unhappily, by trying to coerce your many incompatibilities to function together?

Find ways to make peace in yourself, and to lovingly integrate all that is you. Then you will attract what outwardly reflects the love that you are.

Reflection

Divine Union

In the joyous presence of Aengus, the Celtic god of soulmate love, I proclaim that . . .

I love and accept all that I am.

I appreciate all that has brought me to this place and time.

My masculine and feminine energies joyfully complement each other.

I release any fears I may hold of the masculine.

I release any fears I may hold of the feminine.

I am a Divine Being in complete union with myself.

Use this reflection to come into divine union with yourself.

Paramahansa Yogananda

Paramahansa Yogananda

India & The United States
1893 - 1952

The Father of Western Yoga

In *Autobiography of a Yogi,* Yogananda describes how as a youngster he was drawn to the yogi's life. Ultimately, he became one of the most beloved Hindu gurus in the West and introduced thousands to the practice of yoga, breathwork, meditation and mantras. Yogananda's appeal was based on his blending of eastern and western beliefs to create an inclusive spiritual path.

Yogananda believed that both Krishna and Christ were the Masters from whom his lineage of gurus derived. He said, however, that their way was not the only way. For him, the important goal, shared by all religions, is to love and connect to God. He is an example of how different paths all lead to the same universal truths of love, and a connection to the Divine. He models for us a spiritual path that combines eastern and western belief systems, and shows how we are all one.

The Illusion of Separation

Paramahansa Yogananda's Message

My children, I bring to you this day a message of peace and joy. I thank you for calling upon me to help you transcend your earthly burdens. I can tell you that having peace in your heart, mind, and soul is essential for embodying Unconditional Love. Right now, the unrest and pain in your heart, and the static inside your mind, create barriers to what you seek. And what you truly seek is yourself. Your essence is Unconditional Love. So, hear me when I say that what you are holding onto is stopping you from knowing who you are – the love that you are.

Realize that the world humanity has created is externally oriented. What seems important to you, your main focus in life, is what you have and what you do. Loved ones, these are but seductive illusions that fade away after each lifetime, and often bring discord into your current life. I realize that the chaos in your life is not easy to ignore. The world is filled with perceived drama, pain, hardship, and disappointments. Just open the daily newspaper, or turn on the evening news, and you can find plenty of evidence that peace out in the world is in short supply.

True peace will never be found "out there." Instead, you need to be what you want the world to be; it is that simple, and that difficult. It is found in something you already know. Let go of judgment. Stop trying to determine what is good and bad, and especially, who is good and bad. Things are rarely as they appear, and even your historians disagree about events that played out long ago. Do not burden yourself with the rigidity of right and wrong. This leads to anger and fear, and keeps you apart from the blessings of peace.

I know that judgment has become second nature and occurs as naturally as taking your next breath. Notice what your mind does when you see people who are different from you, or when you witness events that appear to do harm. You've been well-trained by your upbringing and social environment to put things into categories. This creates separation, which is an illusion. We are all connected. We are all expressions of the Divine.

It is now time to transcend the torment of your current thinking, for peace awaits you. Become gently mindful of your thoughts, and what they hold. When thoughts of criticism and divisiveness arise, do not turn on them as bad or evil, but acknowledge what is, and lovingly decide to let them go. Choose differently now. Realize that long-standing patterns do not instantly go away. Continually choose the path to peace; allow it to become your nature.

As you become the peace you wish to see, you will light another match in the illusion of darkness. Be at peace, move forward into your true essence, shine your light of love in the world and throughout creation.

Reflection

Peace and Tranquility

With Yogananda's loving guidance, sit with the following:
I know that . . .

The enduring peace I seek is within me.

My focus is now on my divinity.

I accept that which is not mine to change.

It is not for me to judge the world.

I can immerse myself in the tranquility of Unconditional Love.

Use this practice regularly to bring more peace and tranquility into your daily life.

Highlights of Going Within

The message of these Masters is that in seeking Unconditional Love, we seek what we are. To live this love, we need to let go of our seductive illusions. There is no end to the distractions that can capture our attention. The global or national news, the ongoing political battles near and far, local activities, and the doings of our family and friends all try to steal our peace at times.

The journey inward has been difficult since humans first became aware that there was such a journey. The world seems constructed to lure us away from our true selves. To add to the challenge, we are hard-wired to focus externally because this is where physical threats often exist. Our innate survival instincts are to continuously scan our environment for possible dangers. And, as many of us have discovered, it can be easier to focus on what is "out there" than what is inside.

As we attend to the things of the world, we naturally judge whether they are right or wrong, good or bad. Judging leads us even further away from that which we are, and our judgments can be far from accurate or objective. How often have we judged others — the person who cut us off in traffic, or who has different religious beliefs, or whose cultural practices are foreign to us — without knowing anything about them?

The Masters also pointed out that it serves no purpose to practice self-denial in our quest to be spiritual. Suffering and pain seem to be tenets of many spiritual paths, likely inspired by our understanding of what saints and saviors have endured. Instead of self-denial and suffering, the Masters encourage self-reflection, balance, and acceptance. We are encouraged to go within to know our true selves, and to love and appreciate all of our many facets. To know our true selves, we must see the illusions that we have mistaken for who we are. We can start by recalling times when we have felt the love, power, creativity, and joy that reside within us.

Part I began with three questions:

What can I do to eliminate non-essential distractions in the external world?

What keeps me focused on the world of external events?

Where do I want to place my attention and focus?

Did answers to these questions come to you as you read? Has your awareness of your life expanded as you experienced the Masters' messages? If the majority of your time is directed toward those things outside of yourself, how might you want to shift this, going forward (e.g., daily meditation, self-reflection, breathwork, or connecting to one or more of the Masters)?

Most of us want to feel safe and be informed. In fact, our society values such knowledge. It can be uncomfortable to back away from the daily barrage of news and say, "I don't know," or "I don't need to have an opinion about that." The discomfort may arise within as we endeavor to create emotional space between ourselves and the world. Being distracted by the news, and other non-essentials, can be easier than being with ourselves. Meditation and a commitment to seek Unconditional Love can bring up emotions and larger life questions that are painful to face. They can be difficult to answer, but when we sit with the questions and observe our life, answers will come. Remember, you are not alone on this journey.

Even though I have a twice-daily meditation practice, these Masters helped me become more aware of where I was placing my attention. I can fall prey to analyzing what is going on around me. My professional career included empirical research and using logic to untangle problems. It is easy to apply those investigative skills in the never-ending quest to discover the whys behind my outside world. I've heard teachers, such as Wayne Dyer, speak about the black hole in which the ego would like us to remain. We can spend our lives in this black hole, focused on judging what is right and wrong. This path ultimately leads nowhere, except away from ourselves.

The other message that was illuminating for me in Part 1 is that the spiritual journey is NOT about sacrifice. The message I gleaned from my churchgoing years was that the great spiritual figures suffered a lot. I can still remember being in church when we were called to give ourselves to God and thinking, "Why would I do that?" Lots of these religious icons were either persecuted or, in Jesus' case, crucified. Not an attractive life in my opinion.

While sacrifice and suffering are often viewed as a means to salvation, they can become ends in themselves. *Look at how much I have sacrificed, and how righteous and deserving I am because of it.* They then serve as distractions from the inner journey to love, and they unintentionally feed the ego.

What I have come to appreciate is that the journey within is worth the work of letting go of habitual patterns that keep us from discovering Unconditional Love. As Carl Jung said, "Who looks outside, dreams; who looks inside, awakens." We are being called to look within, to awaken to the truth of who we are, and to know our true self.

Part II
Rising Above

Experiencing Transcendence

Guidance for Reading the Messages in Part II

Rising Above: Experiencing Transcendence is about rising above our current challenges, struggles, and difficulties so that we might better know our true selves. In the following messages, the Masters speak about using such things as joy, gratitude, and forgiveness to elevate our perspective above the day-to-day chaos discussed in Part I.

While enjoying the messages from this group of Masters, you can keep the following questions in mind to help illuminate ways to evolve and transform your life:

How can I apply what the Masters offer to my daily life?

What might I release to experience transcendence?

Is there someone who can help me, or join me, on this journey of transformation?

Krishna

Krishna

India

Mischievous God

In Hinduism, Krishna is believed to be the eighth incarnation of Vishnu, Hinduism's supreme god, and is also a god in his own right. He is known for his compassion, tenderness, and love. Krishna is a being full of life, mischief, and amorous ways, while also recognized for doing heroic deeds. In writings, Krishna is endowed with supernatural abilities: his music can tame rivers and calm storms. His philosophical discussions about life are captured in the great poem, the *Bhagavad-Gita*.

While a notorious lover, Krishna often teaches about the essence of love. He embodies both divine qualities and human frailties just like we do as multidimensional beings. Krishna, like many of the Masters, tells us that death is an illusion, and souls are eternal. He helps us to find the beauty in life.

Finding the Blessings

Krishna's Message

Loved Ones, I come to you with a light heart and a deep hope for your ascension into Unconditional Love. From your perspective, love feels like an intricate puzzle for which you are acquiring the pieces. I can offer you an important one.

Let me begin by saying that it is easy for you to get mired in your current life situation. You have challenges and struggles. You continually solve problems in an attempt to maintain stability. You see difficulties and hardships as threats to your way of life, and you respond to them as such.

I'm here to suggest a different way. Your present way of dealing with life is holding you back from experiencing the joy of life. This joy is one of the keys to Unconditional Love. The pathway to such joy is to find the blessings in your current life – every aspect of it. You may wonder how I can suggest that things like financial hardship and disease can be blessings. My children, they can be if you let them. Financial hardship is a signal to rethink your lifestyle, expenses, or job situation. Physical challenges ask you to reevaluate how you treat your body, or can be a way to exit your body and return to spirit. Often, your difficulties point to your life, or your body, being out of balance.

You are allowed to be upset when you experience pain, and to be unhappy when your life is in turmoil. Even saints can feel angry or upset at what has happened to them. The difference between saints and most humans is that the saints do not wallow in these feelings. They quickly step back to ask: *Why has this occurred? What is the blessing in this situation?*

Much of humanity feels as if every tough situation is punishment for some sin or transgression. It may be hard to believe that you are not being victimized by some judgmental god or unfair system. Virtually everything in your life is here to bring you to the Kingdom of Heaven, which means to live in Unconditional Love no matter what your circumstances might be.

Once you can let go of the emotions generated by each perceived tragedy, I ask you to shift to looking for the blessings. Trust me, they are there, and I am here to help you see them. Call upon me in your darkest hours, and in the midst of your pain and suffering. See me before you, and I will show you the reasons for events and situations in your life, and how those occurrences can benefit you.

The easier it is for you to do this, the easier your life becomes. Imagine shifting from experiencing negativity, fear, and anger to seeing the possibilities and opportunities. This may seem impossible, but I ask you: how many times have you looked back at tragic events and, with the help of hindsight, been able to see them as blessings in disguise? Most people's lives are filled with blessings that were originally perceived as hardships. When you can see the gifts in your challenges as they are happening, you will experience a more joyful way to live.

Find the blessings, Dear Ones. You will then find a key to the Unconditional Love that you are. Know that I am always here to assist you on your journey.

Reflection

The Disguised Blessings

Bringing forth Krishna's joyful and mischievous energy, you can ask him . . .

Help me to see the blessing sooner rather than later.

Help me to know the inherent joy of Unconditional Love.

Help me to see the underlying causes of difficult situations.

Help me to feel the blessings in physical challenges.

Help me to embrace the blessings in relational problems.

Help me to find the blessings and joy in world events.

We often need help to shift and expand our awareness. Let Krishna guide you when you need help.

Babaji

Babaji

India
1861 ~ 1935

Deathless Guru

While his origin is mysterious, Babaji is known as a highly evolved yogi and saint of India who lived for hundreds, or maybe even thousands, of years. Among Babaji's many gifts to humanity is the restoration of the lost art of Kriya Yoga. This form of yoga was disseminated by Babaji's disciple, Lahiri Mahasaya, and then *his* disciple's disciple, Paramahansa Yogananda (who is in Part I).

In *Autobiography of a Yogi*, Paramahansa Yogananda elaborates on Babaji's mission and partnership with Christ. Together, they endeavored to inspire the world to forsake wars, hatred, divisiveness, and materialism. Babaji also believed that any religion or spiritual path can lead to an understanding of God and the three key principles of Truth, Simplicity, and Love.

So, while seen as a saint in India, Babaji's teachings encompass multiple spiritual perspectives consistent with the approach that many of us take on our spiritual journeys. He can inspire us to have the discipline needed to live a life of Unconditional Love.

The Discipline of Love

Babaji's Message

I bow to you, and bid you greetings. I come before you to offer my assistance. It is humbling to be called upon to help those who have come so far on their spiritual journeys. On your journey, I have something for you to consider. I hold the energy of a yogi; I see Unconditional Love from this perspective.

For me, the essence of Unconditional Love is experienced through the discipline, or what you might call steadfastness, of holding love as my ultimate desire. It is not achieved through a set of practices as the term discipline might imply. Unconditional Love is a state of mind, heart, and intent, and thus of total being. It is the spiritual Holy Grail — heaven or nirvana — which can eventually be understood, but is impossible to fully describe. It is The All; and, at the same time, No Thing.

I say becoming one with Unconditional Love comes through a discipline, because there needs to be a primal desire to hold the unholdable. It does not come from a brief desire or hope, but from that which endures through all of life's events. Whether in love or in pain, in joy or in sorrow, the discipline of Unconditional Love remains. This can be most challenging when times are tough and life feels devoid of love. These are the times to call forth that quiet power within you that is your compass.

A key to the power that resides within you is gratitude. Find a handhold of something to be grateful for, feel it, and then find another. There is no end to the things for which you can be grateful, even in the face of great difficulty. Each step of gratitude is a rung on the ladder to lift yourself from the depths of despair. And each step opens wider the doorway to the discipline of Unconditional Love.

The discipline of which I speak is one of flexibility, not rigidity. It is as if you decided to ascend a large mountain, and desired to reach its summit. There are an infinite number of paths to the top, and some will overlap with others on their way upward. No way is better than another, despite what many would like to believe. Many are climbing the mountain of Unconditional Love, and believe they have found the one and only path. This may be humanity's grandest illusion. It is not an illusion you need to share. See the value in all paths; respect all journeys. Join others on their path when it feels appropriate, and strike out on other paths when you feel led to do so.

Imagine those who practice yoga. Be as spiritually flexible as they are physically flexible, while holding steadfast to the intent of being in Unconditional Love. This unwavering intention is your wellspring; hold to it lovingly and gently.

Many believe that discipline is rigid, obeyed like a harsh master. This is unfortunate, for many see the way as too hard and demanding when it is not. Hold to your discipline as if it were precious and delicate, something to be caressed and cherished. If you find you have strayed from your discipline, then lovingly return to it. Do not chide or abuse yourself, but return to it as the grateful lover does who was momentarily called away. The discipline of Unconditional Love always awaits you. It rejoices in your return.

With each return, look to see if you, or your discipline, have changed and may need to come together differently. The discipline of Unconditional Love only asks you to reaffirm your intent and, with an open heart, to look for the path that will move you forward. Sometimes the path will bid you to sit and be still, and other times it will beckon you to change aspects of your life.

The discipline of Unconditional Love, of consistently holding love as your ultimate desire, has the quality of a dynamic flow. The practice, and your experience, of it in your life can be of an infinite variety. It is the soul's lover whose passion and warmth know no bounds.

I will help you find your way if you but ask.

Your loving servant, Babaji

Reflection

Loving Discipline

Call forth Babaji, who represents the possibility of miracles and healing, and ask his assistance to . . .

Release me from the illusion that there is only one true path.

Fuel the quiet desire within that helps me continue the journey of love.

Bring forth the understanding of Unconditional Love that transcends words.

Gently guide me back to the journey of Unconditional Love when I stray.

Know love as my ultimate desire.

The discipline of love improves our lives in so many ways.

Let Babaji help you create the discipline that will bring more love and joy into your life.

Commit to the discipline of regularly connecting with the Masters.

Maitreya

Maitreya

Asia

The Mysterious One

Maitreya is seen as the future Buddha whose teachings lead away from cravings and materialism (which create suffering) and, instead, encourages humans to follow the dharma. The dharma is often understood as the universal force in creation. It is also a way of living in alignment with the right way of behaving. It is a cornerstone of many Indian religious and spiritual traditions, including Buddhism, Hinduism, Jainism, and Sikhism.

Maitreya is viewed by some as a highly-regarded member of what is called the *Spiritual Hierarchy* believed to be the Masters of Wisdom, and by others as a member of the brotherhood that includes Jesus, Saint Germain, and Archangel Michael (the latter two are in Part III). Like these three Masters, Maitreya is believed to be a spirit who will incarnate in the future, achieve total enlightenment, and teach the pure dharma to humankind.

Maitreya reminds us of the sacredness of laughter, play, and joy in our spirituality.

Let Joy Guide Your Way

Maitreya's Message

I come to you today with a joy that knows no bounds. It springs from the very heartbeat of creation, and it is here for you to draw upon for your journey to Unconditional Love. Let love be the vehicle that transforms your life, and let joy guide your way. It is possible to know this joy in every breath, every kindness, every color, every thought, and every movement. Why is joy so important? It is important because Unconditional Love and joy are handfasted throughout all of eternity. One does not exist without the other; it is a spiritual marriage. Heavy minds and hearts can study the nuances of love from now until the end of time and fail to know it. But notice what happens to your entire being when you are joyful. You feel better, your body functions well, and you look better. Everything is different when joy is your state of being.

For many, joy can feel frivolous or unjustified. They will argue that with so much going on in their lives and in the world, how can they possibly live in joy? My answer is that joy isn't out there; it comes from how you view your world and, thus, emanates from within. Discover the joys of life: your own heartbeat, nature as it comes alive in spring and lets go in fall, the ability to pay a bill, talking to a friend, a few minutes of quiet, or a favorite song on the radio.

So too, your world is filled with endless miracles for which to be grateful: the miracle of life, of nature, of flight, of your own body, of earth hurtling through space, of the vast cosmos, and of subatomic particles. It is no wonder the Buddha has a perpetual smile. Look beyond your worries and your challenges, for they only bring you more of the same. Your life and world are filled with wonders. See them, feel them, and know them, and then watch what happens.

Joy is what fuels the opening of your heart. Joy allows you to dislodge the pain and suffering you have stored inside. Let joy be like the warm sun in spring that melts away the winter ice. Everything, from life's hardships to its disappointments that have hardened like ice in your soul, can be thawed with joy.

Shifting into complete joy can feel impossible – so start a little at a time. Today, notice one or two things that bring a spark of joy. It can be the feeling of a pet, the flight of a bird overhead, or a shaft of sunlight through the clouds. Then smile.

In subsequent days, look for more and more that is joyous. Then later, look for it in those less obvious things and events.

Feel the joy when countries of the world respond with aid to major disasters, or when you find something a bit easier to do than it was the day before. Eventually, you will know the joy of all existence, that everything is lovable, and it will help you open the door of Unconditional Love that you may have closed long ago.

In joy, I bid you farewell for now. But like all of the Masters, you need only call on me to join you. When you are having difficulty knowing joy – call me. When situations seem to lack all joy – call me. I will share with you my view, and through my sight, you will see and know the joy of all creation.

Reflection

Joy

With Maitreya as a loving companion, who can help you use the power of joy, ask for the following:

To know joy in every breath, kindness, and thought I experience.

To know that joy and love are inseparable.

To feel joy emanate from within me.

To use joy to release my pain and suffering.

To allow joy to reveal the miracles that abound in my life.

To let joy guide me to awakening to love.

This practice can create powerful shifts in your life.

White Tara

White Tara

Asia

The Mother of Compassion

White Tara is a part of the Buddhist, Hindu, Jainist, and Tibetan Tantric spiritual traditions. She is known as a protector of her followers, who call upon her for courage and to overcome fear and obstacles.

As White Tara, she is serene and embodies the perfection and wisdom that lead to spiritual joy and to nirvana. She is considered the Mother of Compassion. She is often shown with a third eye (for clairvoyance), playing a lute, or holding a lotus. She is always adorned with jewels, and may be dressed and crowned as a Bodhisattva — a being who has earned the right to ascend into enlightenment, but who chooses to stay to help all others attain enlightenment. She offers to watch over us and bring us peace.

Again, we encounter a Master who embodies joy as a dimension of enlightenment, and as a key to rising above. White Tara also reminds us of the power of "fire" to purify and transform our lives.

The Fire of Purification

White Tara's Message

Dear Ones, you want to know about Unconditional Love? I am the one who represents the energy of purification. The opportunity to speak to you brings me great joy. Even the thought of it opens and warms my heart. From my perspective, love is about revealing oneself without shame or hesitation. The love of which I speak is completely bold, yet vulnerable at the same time.

I know you have attempted to remove passion and notions of sensuality from your pursuit of Unconditional Love. You might be surprised by my telling you to bring them back after you have purified yourself of misconceptions. Once you can truly let go of your false self-images and fears, then you can come full circle to being wonderfully, unabashedly and sensually in love with yourself and others. You can then be like the lover that only sees the good in all that is called life.

What is this purification process that will allow you to rediscover the totality of being in love? It is the process of mindfulness. Every time your mind brings up fear, anger, hate, or judgment, bring it to my cold fire of purification. Imagine holding these thoughts or feelings in your cupped hands; bless them for coming forth to be released. See my fire ignite before you, and release what you are holding into the flames. Let the fire of purification transform these issues into light and love. Then step into the flames yourself, and let the fire purify you as well.

Fear not these flames; they do not burn, as they are merely a symbol. The real purification comes from the desire in your heart. As you step into the fire, give thanks, and feel the shift as your burdens are released. Over time, there will be less and less to purify, and more that you can love. The moment will come when you realize that you are very much in love with yourself in a way that may now seem impossible. It is not the love of the narcissist. It is, instead, the lover who loves all of you, deeply and completely.

While many might want to use this purification process slowly, I offer you other, more efficient paths if you so choose. Find a time where you can be still and connect to your highest power. This might be Source, God, Buddha, Krishna, Christ, or another divine being that represents the highest form of love, for you. Feel the complete love and acceptance this being has for you. Then ask your spiritual guides to remove everything that is holding you back from being Unconditional Love.

When this has been done, call upon me to bring the fire of purification. All those assembled, including yourself, will fuel this fire into a great blaze. Then gather up in your hands all those unloving things, and step into the flames. Do this with complete joy and gratitude. Feel yourself letting go of all those things that are ready for release. Once again, do not fear the fire, for it does not burn. Let the flames tickle away all those concerns and burdens, and experience the process of falling totally in love with all of you.

You can do this as many times as you wish. Each time, call upon your deity of love, your guides, and me, and we will support you through this process. Know that you are blessed, for there are many who await your transcendence.

With my love and passion,

White Tara

Reflection

Purification

White Tara embodies the courage to overcome our fears, and the wisdom to know spiritual joy. With her gentle fire of purification, ask her . . .

To help me embrace the purification process.

To help me release my misconceptions of Unconditional Love.

To help me release my misconceptions of myself.

To reveal myself without shame.

To know the true desires of my heart.

To be the lover that sees the truth in myself and others.

To bring forth the passion of Unconditional Love into my life.

This practice will help you release all that is not you so you can rise above.

Parvati

Parvati

India

Hindu Goddess of Motherhood

The story of Parvati, daughter of the mountain, is thought to have started with the tribes of the Himalayas. In Hinduism, she is the Mother goddess. In the Shakti religion, she encompasses the energy of the entire universe while representing the unity of all things — something many of us are striving to experience.

From an early age, Parvati set her sights on marrying Shiva, the Hindu god of both creation and destruction. The couple became known for their passion; their embrace frequently shook the world. Parvati is often depicted within a contented family or embracing Shiva, representing her role as Shakti, generator of his power. She may also be seen holding Ganesh, her son (whose message is next).

Although she carries the power and energy of Shiva's austerity to the earth, she is also seen as the goddess of fertility, motherhood, and devotion to one's spouse. Thus, she can help us birth the Divine in ourselves, and step into what we are meant to do in this lifetime. Parvati knows the shadow side of life, and can help us use it as a powerful tool for transformation.

Loving the Shadow

Parvati's Message

I am here to speak of change, so that you may better know
and experience the love of self. Change is not what you on
earth often believe it to be. To you, positive change involves
transforming bad habits into ones that are better, or more
socially acceptable, such as quitting smoking and taking
up exercise. Some of you view positive change as creating a
life for yourself that conforms to current moral and health
standards. This ignores the reality that ALL experiences have
value, whether you currently view them as good or bad.
Viewing habits as bad, or feelings as negative, simply pushes
them into your shadow side. You may, on the surface, appear
to be completely different from those undesired aspects, but
you are far from being free of them.

The most powerful change you can make is to love
yourself — all of yourself, not just the admirable parts. The
first step in total self-love is to accept that everything about
you has value. Every quality, characteristic, and personality
trait has a purpose. Each one shows you who you truly are,
and helps you become what you really want to be. Believe it
or not, you have chosen the life you are now experiencing,

including your personality, circumstances, and those who surround you.

There is nothing wrong with changing your life; I am all about change. The critical part of change is the motivation and desire that drive it. For example, losing weight to be more socially accepted pushes the fat portion of yourself into your shadow. This shadow aspect remains a primary driver of your life, regardless of how thin you appear. On the surface, you've made a positive change, but the underlying self-rejection or hatred can persist. From my higher vantage point, not much change has taken place except for your outward appearance.

So how can you make changes from a more loving perspective? Here is what I suggest. The more you are an observer of your life, and the less you are an evaluator, the better your vantage point will be. You will be better able to appreciate all that you have experienced, and better able to see and understand what is bringing situations into your life. Then you can determine what changes to make, and what shifts need to come about, to attract different situations and people to you.

It is often said that doing the same thing over and over again, and expecting different results is insane. How often have you been able to look back and see that holding a certain belief has led to similar outcomes, no matter how much you tried to create a different result? If a man believes in his heart that all women cannot be trusted, what do you think is going to manifest within all of his relationships? No matter whether he dates a doctor, lawyer, or accountant, he will most assuredly still find that his partner will prove his belief to be correct. Only by becoming more of an observer in his life will this man discover his role in what he is experiencing. He does, however, have the choice to continue to believe as he has in the past, and thus continue to experience the untrustworthy side of all his mates.

Letting go of beliefs and feelings is not an easy task, as you no doubt know. Usually when we think we have changed or let go of something, what we have really done is to shove it into our shadow side. This just creates more problems.

Instead, let me offer you a paradoxical alternative. It is easier to let go of something you love than to let go of something you hate or fear. These feelings keep you tied to what you wish to eliminate.

Love allows us the emotional space, and compassion, to make the adjustments we desire. Love gently dislodges the anchor that has held us in place. It eliminates the self-recrimination that would send the anchor back down to hold us fast again.

Please give this some thought, my children, and go with my blessings.

Reflection

Your Shadow

Parvati's perspective of bringing forth the new, and her devotion to love, helps us to emerge from our shadows. With her sight, ask her to help you with each of the following.

Sit with each one as long as is needed.

To see the value in all of my experiences.

To shine the light of love into my shadow.

To embrace this life and body I've chosen.

Being a loving observer of myself.

Seeing the patterns and habits that no longer serve me.

Revisit this, and call upon Parvati to help you, as often as you need.

Ganesh

Ganesh

India

Hindu God of Wisdom & Learning

Ganesh (Ganesha, Ganesa, Ganapati), the son of Parvati, is depicted with an elephant head because his original head was cut off while defending his mother. He is a friendly and good-natured deity, and very popular in Hindu culture. He represents the joy, fun and lightness in overcoming obstacles, and is associated with success and abundance. His followers see him as a benefactor who uses his trunk to remove obstacles for them, ensuring success and abundance.

Ganesh's head symbolizes the soul and denotes wisdom, his trunk represents the universal OM, and his body personifies earthly existence. He is usually depicted with only one full tusk. It is said that while conversing with the poet Vyasa, Ganesh hastily broke off one of his tusks, and wrote down the *Mahabharata* as Vyasa told it to him. This is the longest known epic poem in the world. It includes the great poem known to many as the *Bhagavad-Gita*. For this reason, Ganesh is thought of as a patron of literature, and also as a god of wisdom, writing, and art. Students and creative types call upon him.

Ganesh, and his joy and lightness, can help us know how and when to say no, and how and when to say yes, on our spiritual journey.

The Power of Yes and No

Ganesh's Message

Unconditional Love is all about possibilities and opening up to new realms of your own being. It takes a fearless joy that is willing to explore all of the wonderful recesses of your soul. It is about saying yes to life and to yourself, about affirming your aliveness with wonder at all of creation, and about being willing to be transformed in every moment.

What stops you from living in Unconditional Love? Your fears and patterns are what stop you. Fear puts things out of bounds; it defines your spiritual territory, and then patterns develop, which make it easy to stay there. What is it that makes you feel unworthy to shine your light? You may believe you must hide your supposed flaws, or your beliefs in original sin. Do you think you have done harm in this or other lifetimes? If so, it can feel impossible to stand before your god at life's end and feel worthy. The result is that your patterns become your cages, and your fears become your wardens.

The patterns you enact every day came into being to make your life easier. In many ways, they have succeeded too well. They reduce the effort and thought of your daily life. How you function throughout the day is a progression from one pattern to another until the day is done. Patterns have served us well, yet when we become captives to them, they no longer serve, they control.

What do you desire, or want to say *yes* to, but will have trouble saying *yes* to, because of your patterns? You've received many suggestions for more fully becoming Unconditional Love. Where does getting quiet or meditating fit with the hectic patterns of your life? Where do you put the time to spend with the Masters in your well-patterned life schedule?

Like Yin and Yang, *yes* carries the complementary energy of *no*. There are times when saying *no* makes it possible to then say *yes*. Is it *no* to being less than divine, or *no* to being drawn into others' drama? There are other *nos* you may need to employ to withdraw from the myriad distractions in your life, and to the self-criticism that plays in your mind.

No is a powerful word, and one to use with caution. *No* in the form of rejection simply pushes each issue aside and into your shadow to fester. The *no* that I speak of carries the gentle energy of a heartfelt *no thank you*. It acknowledges what is being offered, and often why it is being offered, and gently chooses an alternative.

These are the *nos* that lead to the *yeses* that take us to the love we seek. The gentle and appreciative *no* opens the space for the *yes*. It does this through its understanding of how our choices and patterns have served us in the past. It does not charge what we are releasing with things like anger and disdain. It brings things to our consciousness so we can make more heart-centered choices.

Give yourself permission to let go of distractions so you can experience your joy, your passion, and your desire. Tune into the positivity and buoyancy of *yes* — the *yes* that encompasses your entire being. Say the word *yes* and feel its power flow through you. Say *yes* to your hopes and dreams, and *no* to the limiting thoughts that can immediately follow. Say *yes* to your highest good, and send this forth with love and appreciation. Say *yes* to joy, hope, beauty, tenderness, and miracles. Feel the shift that takes place.

You are more than welcome to say *yes* to me, and I will joyfully guide you on your journey. It would be my honor and pleasure.

Reflection

Saying No, Saying Yes

With the help of the happy, abundant, and good-natured Ganesh, we can ponder these from his message:

To know the loving self-affirmation of No.

To release the patterns and fears holding me in place.

To know the positivity, buoyancy, and power of Yes.

To know and appreciate all the possibilities before me.

To know the fearless joy that allows me to explore my entire being.

To practice the mindfulness that leads to a less mind-driven life.

Let Ganesh help you use No and Yes to create a solid foundation upon which to grow Unconditional Love in your life.

Quan Yin

Quan Yin

Asia

Goddess of Generosity

In Buddhism, Quan Yin is believed to have achieved enlightenment, but instead of ascending fully into spirit, she has chosen to remain connected to the earth to aid humanity. Thus, she is considered a Bodhisattva. She is beloved for her compassion and assistance to those who seek her help, and revered for her innocence, purity and spirituality. Her name means "she who hears the weeping world." She is the most popular figure in Buddhism and is often compared to Mother Mary of the Christian world.

Beautiful and supremely serene, Quan Yin can be depicted with many arms (often cited as a thousand), representing her ability to aid, protect and intercede.

Quan Yin asks for no offerings, unlike many other Asian deities. She is gracious and generous with her aid, granting fertility to newlyweds, healing the sick, and offering protection from storms, floods, fires, and lightning. Prisoners ask her for their freedom, and students seek help with their exams. She guards temples, bringing peace to those who meditate upon her name.

Forward or Backward?

Quan Yin's Message

What would you ask of me this day, for I bring to you a message of love. All of you carry many burdens, and your hearts are heavy. What concerns and fears do you hold close that are weighing you down and holding you back from the unfolding joy of existence? Are they financial, physical, relational, or concerns for the world or all of creation? There is no end to the things you can fret about in your life, in the lives of your loved ones, in your country, and in your world. This has been the case throughout time, and this won't be changing anytime soon. But worrying has never solved these problems, and it won't work now either.

Feeding the world with the energies of worry, anger, regret, and hopelessness only serves to preserve what you least desire. In every moment, you have a choice about how you react to what is unfolding in your life. My suggestion is: to that which brings you pain – send love. The things you fear – send them love. Then release them to me, or to whatever Master or Divine Being you choose.

You may say that this isn't possible. How could you send love, and then release what lays so heavy on your heart? It is your choice. Do as you have done, and stay bound to your fights and fears; or, love them and let them go. Feel what your world would be like without all of your burdens. What would it be like to heal the emotional scars you now own as parts of your identity? Inside you may be screaming that you cannot do this, that justice won't be served, retribution is due, and that you have the right to feel injured. Yes, you do, if this is what you truly want. But I ask you: to what end? How have all of these wounds and grievances served you? Or do they hold you back? How much of your identity is bound up in past abuse, suffering, or pain? Such an identity will never allow you to flourish.

If I told you to drive your automobile forward by looking only in the rearview mirror, how well would that work? Are you not doing much the same emotionally, energetically, and spiritually as you move through your life? How often have you crashed time and again into emotional objects that were from your past?

Release yourself by letting go. It is not, as it may feel, like giving up. It is the opposite. It is seizing hope where there has been despair, holding joy where there has been pain, knowing peace where there has been fear, and feeling gratitude where there has been anger. A new life awaits you; it is your choice.

Rise above all that cannot be changed, accept the world for what it is, and find the subtle miracle in each moment. I can help you do this if you wish it to be so. For now, know that I am with you.

Reflection

Releasing the Past

Quan Yin is a deity of endless generosity and compassion. She has a deep desire to help us see more clearly what we are holding onto, and how we might move forward. With her loving support, ask her for insight into . . .

Knowing the truth about my ideas of justice.

Knowing the truth about my grievances and my need for retribution.

Seeing the truth of my worries, anger, and regrets.

Healing the emotional scars that are parts of my identity.

Releasing my pain and my fear.

Shifting my focus from the past to the present.

Sending love to all parts of myself.

Call upon Quan Yin whenever you need compassion for yourself or for others.

Highlights of Rising Above

In Part II, the Masters show us that by accepting what is, and who we are, we can rise above pain and suffering. We can experience a life of joy and the essence of Unconditional Love. The Masters point out the power of finding the blessings in what has unfolded in our lives, as well as the importance of feeling gratitude. They suggest that we can do this by being loving and gentle observers of our lives through the practice of mindfulness, which comes from Buddhism.

One theme that runs through these messages is that things that may have once seemed incompatible do coexist. Seeming opposites work together as part of the whole: discipline is flexible; our shadows need the light; *yes* also needs *no*. These Masters ask us to expand our vision and take the bird's eye view. And when we do this, we see that all is as it should be; there is no need to judge, since, in time, more will be revealed.

One potential surprise in these messages is the idea that joy and love are inexorably connected, and that joy can fuel the opening of our hearts. Maitreya went so far as to say, "You cannot enter the kingdom of Heaven with a heavy heart." This is quite different from many traditional notions of spirituality that require a solemn austerity in order to earn a place in Heaven. How many spiritual pursuits have required self-denial, sacrifice, and suffering to attain its idea of being spiritually worthy? No hair shirts, self-flogging, or simulated crucifixions demanded here.

Instead, the Masters advocate being gentle with oneself and others, creating joy by becoming aware of the miracles and gifts in our lives, returning to love whenever possible, and releasing everyone — including ourselves — from the grip of judgment. White Tara even provides a way to painlessly purify ourselves when things like fear and anger arise by using the fire of purification.

At the beginning of Part II, three questions were provided for consideration. The first question was: *How can I apply what the Masters offer to my daily life?* This is a critical question for all of us. What from the Masters resonated with you? Which practices do you have a desire to incorporate into your life?

After deciding what you want to change, there is the challenge of figuring out how to change it. This brings us to the next question: *What might I let go of in order to experience transcendence?* Letting go of anything that is not love is a great place to start. Creating the time and emotional space to embrace gratitude, forgiveness, and compassion helps us to rise above the things that are holding us back.

We can also benefit from contact with others: fellow journeyers, spiritual teachers, and mentors. Although the Masters emphasize becoming more mindful of our own reactions and feelings (Part 1), they do not suggest that we try to do everything on our own. The third question, therefore, asked: *Is there someone who can help me, or join me, on this journey of transformation?* Who can help you at this time, and how might he or she be a part of the joy and gratitude that is central to unconditional love? Help can come in many forms. Maybe it is to help us keep a desired meditation schedule, provide feedback about our responses, or serve as a role model.

One of the most important messages here for me is gratitude. It has been too easy to remember the hard times and challenges. While I might feel begrudgingly grateful that I survived, this is never enough. A dear friend often asks me, "Don, how did that situation benefit you, and what have you been able to bring forth because you had that experience?" In essence, how did choosing to have that experience aid me in where I am today? With very difficult past events, my first reaction might be negative but, if I'm willing to look beyond that veil, there are always gifts that await me.

I have also tended to make this journey hard work. Isn't this serious stuff? I know only too well how to be serious when tackling what seem like problems. What I have often missed is the sheer joy that comes with each step and new realization. This is where I have received lots of help. That same friend will look at me and, barely containing her enthusiasm, prod me to feel the miracle that is taking place. The people in our lives are there for a reason.

Part III
Living in the Light

Emerging From Our Shadows

Guidance for Reading
the Messages in Part III

The Masters in Part III help us with exactly what Jung directs us to do: "mak[e] the darkness conscious." They call for us to emerge from the hiding places we've created in an attempt to feel safe. They offer their assistance so that we can more fully become the divine energy of love for the benefit of the world.

Stepping out of the shadows means facing our fears. The following questions might serve to guide you on your journey:

How can I come to love and accept all of me?

What are my greatest fears in stepping forward?

What do I most want to contribute to the world in this lifetime?

How can I summon the strength that I need to move forward?

Archangel
Michael

Archangel Michael

Omnipresent

Prince of Light

In Christian, Jewish, and Islamic traditions, Archangel Michael ("who is as God" in Hebrew) is recognized as preeminent among all angels. Today, Michael is known as a protector and a dispeller of fear and evil. He is called upon to assist with one's courage and true purpose in life. Many have turned to Michael in their hour of need because he symbolizes enduring strength in the midst of adversity. Joan of Arc said that Michael inspired her in battle during the Hundred Years' War. Moses credited him with leading the Israelites toward the promised land.

Archangel Michael is often depicted as a tall, handsome, magnificent, winged angel who wields a brilliant sword. Pictures of him often show light emanating from both his sword and his entire being. He radiates the light and love of God. As the "Prince of Light," he embodies the struggle between light and dark. Again, we have a Master who personifies the opposing aspects of being human, and serves as a reminder of our own divine nature.

Your Divine Reflection

Archangel Michael's Message

You know me as a protector and guardian, and many have called upon me in their moment of need. Now there is a need to manifest on earth that which you call Unconditional Love, for its absence poses the ultimate challenge to humanity. I am speaking of a love that values all the wonders on your planet, and delights in the very essence of existence.

My sword has been used to protect and bring forth all that is meant to be. Now is the time for you to take your rightful place with me in raising up true love as the most powerful force on earth. This will happen by freeing yourself of your limited view of who and what you are, by emerging out of the shadows of your false identity, and by rising into the light. Love is who you are, but this truth has been covered up by your flawed self-image. You have placed me, and other ascended Masters, above yourself because you feel unworthy to take flight with us. You feel inferior to those you see as angelic beings, Masters, and gods. This is not truth.

The shift on earth starts with you. It happens when you come to know yourself, love yourself, and spread your wings. You cannot raise the earth's vibration through anger, or by being upset with the way things are. You cannot bring about your heart's desire through fighting and strife. Heaven on earth starts in your heart. So, what will it take for you to remove the walls from around your heart that fear has built? It will take knowing, with complete certainty, that you are divine; that you are a being of light and love. We, who you put on high, await your ascension to join us.

I know that what I ask is not easy. Your identity is bound to the world, and the energetic pain and fear of many challenging lifetimes run strong and deep. But now is the time, like no other, to step out of your self-created encasement. All that has occurred has brought you to this place of longing and understanding. It is not about being more successful, attractive, or prosperous. It is about a knowing that transcends time and space.

It is not about following any set of religious practices or spiritual steps. These can help you for a while, but they are not who you are. The Masters, Source itself, and I all mirror who you truly are, for you are beyond measure, and we beckon you to join the great awakening that is now unfolding. We would joyfully lead you back to your true identity.

Just as I have been the beacon for justice, you will be the beacon for the ideals — be they love, compassion, or peace

— that are your heart's desire. Force none, push none, and potentially attract all. Be such a beacon, not to prove others wrong or less, but do it simply to express who you are. Expect not perfection, for the perfection you have pursued does not exist. In this realm of three-dimensional reality, you will always face challenges and opportunities. Yet, all is as it needs to be.

You may have called on me in the past for protection, and you may continue to do so. Know that you can also call upon me to help you discover your true essence. Call on me in your meditations and quiet periods. Ask me to come to you, and to reflect back to you that which you are. What you see of me will be a mirror of you. If you see my wings, then know you are of the angelic realm. If you feel my strength, then know that you are strong. What stands out about me will allow you to better understand yourself. Know that you, like every being, have a role in the transformation taking place. It does not matter whether you are a king or a beggar. As we spend time together, you will come to more readily accept the truth of who you are, and ultimately that you are love.

I am with you always.

Reflection

The Light of Your Divinity

Archangel Michael, who is known as "The Prince of Light" and the dispeller of fear and evil, is here to help us on our journey of healing. Imagine him coming to you in all of his brilliance. See his radiance and the light streaming from his sword. Ask him . . .

Please show me who I truly am.

Show me my reflection in your eyes.

Help me to feel my divinity.

How can I more fully spread my wings and soar?

Help me know my role in the transformation of the world.

Let Michael's brilliant light fill your heart and your life.

Amaterasu

Amaterasu

Japan

Shinto Sun Goddess

Amaterasu is the sun goddess, and the principal deity of the Shinto religion. Gentle and loving, she rules all of the Shinto deities. She teaches us the healing power of laughter and the wisdom of humor. It is believed that the Japanese emperors are her descendants. The Japanese flag still carries her symbol — the rising sun. Of all the world's large, contemporary religions, Amaterasu is the only primary deity who is female.

Legend has it that Amaterasu retreated to a cave where she sealed the entrance to avoid her abusive brother, the storm god. Thus, devoid of her light, the world went completely dark. Eventually, the other gods and goddesses hatched a plan to lure her out. They did so with joy and gaiety. Amaterasu relented, and brought her brilliant light back into the world. Many of us have done the same as Amaterasu — we have hidden our light from the world.

The Beauty of the Shadow
Amaterasu's Message

You have come to ask me about Unconditional Love. Ah, what a wondrous topic. I embody the energy of stepping forward into the light. This is necessary to be in Unconditional Love. When you are in this state of love, hiding is not only unnecessary, but also not possible.

Many of you are afraid to step out of your self-imposed shadows. You don't like how you look. You lack confidence in what you have to say, or you fear what will happen when you do speak your truth. You project the small "you" to feel safe. Given how the world has responded to you and your truth throughout many lifetimes, this is not surprising. Yet, it does not serve you, or the world, to play small, and it is time to set yourself free of the bonds of your shadow.

Presently you may be confused about how to do this. You've invested so much energy in hiding your true identity that it can be difficult to let it emerge. I encourage you to do what much of your instincts tell you *not* to do. This may be giving voice to the gentle truths that reside within, or allowing yourself to shine and be seen. I am here not only to assist you, but also to challenge you.

Call upon me, and I will hold up a mirror to your soul. I will show you the magnificence within you, and help you to see yourself with divine eyes. I will also help you to accept and appreciate the physical vessel you have chosen for this lifetime.

My sacred job, loved ones, is to help you see your beauty. My mirror does not lie. By coming to accept and appreciate yourself, you will unlock the ability to see this in everyone else. You can then play my role for them by helping them see their own magnificence. This is what Unconditional Love does.

It starts with you. Step out of the shadows of limitation. Come into the light of love. Shine your light for all of creation and enjoy life at a new level. Go with my blessings!

Reflection

Shining Light on the Shadow

In your mind's eye, bring forth the shining countenance of Amaterasu, the sun goddess. Ask that joy and the warmth of her sun fill your entire being. Once you can feel this, ask her to help you to . . .

Emerge from hiding.

No longer project the "small me" into the world.

Accept and appreciate my physical vessel.

Accept and appreciate others' physical vessels.

See the total beauty of who I am.

See the total beauty of all others.

Call upon this joyous Sun Goddess anytime you need light.

Mother Mary

Mother Mary

Judea

18 BCE ~ 33 AD

Mother Mary

Mother Mary is much-loved across multiple faiths. Her loving and gentle countenance has provided comfort and support to many. We have little information about her life, though bits of her story are mentioned in the four Gospels of the New Testament. We are told that Mary was a young Jewish woman from Nazareth who was betrothed to Joseph when the archangel Gabriel came to her, and told her she was to bear the Son of God. This child was to be conceived by agency of the Holy Spirit, making Mary the Virgin Mother.

Some modern faiths believe that Mary and young Jesus spent time in Qumran studying with the Essenes, a learned Jewish sect. It is also believed that Mary and Jesus received initiations in the temples of Egypt. The Essenes may have been the authors of the Dead Sea Scrolls.

Over the centuries, many Christians have viewed Mary as a loving mother figure who intercedes on their behalf, making their relationship with her very personal. Devotion to Mary has also been fueled by the many reported visions of her worldwide. Many cathedrals and churches are dedicated to her.

Mary can help us as we strive to open ourselves to the power of Unconditional Love, while also feeling safe.

Vulnerability and Boundaries

Mother Mary's Message

Loved Ones, where do I begin with such a wonderful topic as Unconditional Love? You are at a point in your evolution where you may know in your hearts that the time is now. I have come to offer my love and support, as well as to open another pathway for you.

I can speak to something that humanity has struggled with throughout the ages — vulnerability. Many who step into the energy of Unconditional Love feel stripped of their protection. This happens because Unconditional Love is revealing. It illuminates who we are as we emerge from the shadows into the light. We can feel things we have tried to avoid. We can feel exposed, and porous to outside influences.

The problem facing you on earth is your layers of fear. Exposing who you are opens up the possibility of ridicule and rejection, so you hide the parts of yourself that might engender such responses. The openness of Unconditional Love also means not shielding yourselves from all that is taking place. Can you be in Unconditional Love and be okay at the same time?

You will come to understand that Unconditional Love means vulnerability, as in transparency; it does not mean being without boundaries. It means coming to loving terms with yourselves so you can let yourselves, and others, see you without feeling fear or shame. It means becoming loving observers of life, instead of being emotionally bound up in all that takes place in your lives and in your world. It does not mean walling off your emotions. It's all about acceptance, not rejection. It's about choosing where and when to get involved, instead of trying to do and be everything. It's about knowing and accepting your and others' limitations.

Humanity has struggled with the seeming paradox of vulnerability and boundaries. On the surface, they appear mutually exclusive; they are not. Vulnerability within the context of Unconditional Love is the willingness to reveal who you are. If there are aspects of you that you feel you need to hide – why? Is what you are hiding viewed as socially unacceptable? My question to you, Dear Ones, is: what is the cost of being accepted? If you could fully and completely accept yourself, would it matter?

There are things you can fear about yourselves. Many have tremendous anger buried deep inside from lifetimes of hardship and abuse. You can also fear your power to harm and destroy. There can be feelings or desires that no longer serve you. What do you do with these? You acknowledge and heal them. Come to understand that every being on this planet has a shadow side — those things they loathe or fear. Your willingness to illuminate and heal your shadow enables others to do the same.

Becoming comfortable with yourselves, and lovingly addressing those things you want to change, allows for the vulnerability and visibility of Unconditional Love. It also helps you to set boundaries that are in your highest good. As the ancient saying goes, "Love thy neighbor as thyself." Often, you are more protective of others than of yourselves. Unconditional Love is not the sacrifice of self, any more than it is the sacrifice of others. It is an affirmation of your divinity, and your journey. It is about ascension, miracles, and hope.

You know the story of Joseph and me protecting Jesus from being killed as a child. We protected him, and we protected ourselves. To do otherwise was not in the highest good. How many times have you chosen to do what was not in your highest good because you felt pressure from others, or because of your own guilt? It is time now to love yourself as you have loved others, for loving yourself is the key to true love for all. Shouldering the burdens of others does not serve them, or you; it only forestalls their lessons and holds you back.

I love you more than you can imagine, and I know what I have asked of you is not easy. As you contemplate and meditate on Unconditional Love, invite me to join you. I will help you feel the openness, the strength, and the acceptance of Unconditional Love. The doorway to yourself, and the love of Source, is here for you when you are ready. Honor me as your friend and guide. Know that you have spent lifetimes preparing for this time on earth.

With all of my love, I await you.

Reflection

Vulnerability

For many of us, Mary is the essence of the Divine Mother. In the presence of her love, her gentleness, and her unwavering support, ask her for help.

Mary, please help me to . . .

Know the truth about vulnerability.

Lovingly address those things about me I want to change.

Release the layers of fear I hold.

Release feelings and desires that no longer serve me.

Come to loving terms with myself.

Emerge from my shadow.

Become a loving observer of life.

Love comes from our authentic self, which can only exist when we embrace our vulnerability. Use this reflection regularly to help you become more authentically yourself.

Mother Earth

Mother Earth

Gaia

Mother Earth, also known as the Greek goddess Gaia, has many names: Asherah, the mother goddess of Canaan; Ishtar, the Mesopotamian goddess of fertility; and Isis, the Egyptian goddess of the feminine ideal. These goddesses usually represent some or all of the characteristics of fertility, motherhood, creation and nature.

Mother Earth has gifted us with her love, sustenance, and the great beauty of our home, and there is a growing awareness and appreciation for her. As the Greek goddess Gaia (4000 BCE - 400 AD) she gave birth to the sea, to the mountains, and to time itself. She birthed a new generation of deities followed by the human race.

In response to demands to give up their way of life, and to the damage to our planet, many Native Americans have spoken of "Mother Earth" in metaphorical terms. The Indian chief, Tecumseh, referred to earth as his mother; and, many Native Americans, as well as environmental activists, use the term "Mother Earth." She is viewed as a living being supporting us, and worthy of our love and respect.

Many Expressions of Love

Mother Earth's Message

I am your home, your support, your playground, your school, and your mother. I have known you since you were birthed in earthly form. I've watched you struggle, triumph, suffer, rejoice, love, and hate. You've built, and you've destroyed. All along, you have discovered and contributed to all of creation.

Now you are ready for a major step in our combined evolution. This is moving into the realm of Unconditional Love. You have many of the pieces. It is time to put them together and to live them. I take great delight in helping you; and, in so doing, ascending with you. You are my children, who now realize that you are co-creators.

I have loved you unconditionally, although it might not have felt so. At my core, I am molten energy — fiery and passionate. This enduring aspect of me is similar to the love that powers creation. You do not live in my core, physically; you inhabit the surface. Yet, you do live in my core in the same way your loved ones live in your heart.

My love for you is expressed in infinite ways, from the ice at my poles, to the tropics on my center, to the countless varieties of terrain, vegetation, and animals. My love, and the core of my being, has been steadfast and ever-changing. I've created everything from lush paradises to devastating environmental challenges. You, as humanity, have chosen all manner of places and ways to live on me. Through it all, you have made your own decisions about how to best use me for your collective experiences.

Have I always agreed with your choices? No. Have I grieved when there has been wholesale slaughter? Yes. But I have never punished you for those choices. My love for you is unconditional. I exist so you can experience all that the physical realm has to offer.

It may be difficult to understand how my love could be expressed in so many ways, and yet, be all a part of the same love. How could it be that I express my love in sunshine and soft rain, as well as in hurricanes, volcanoes and floods? It is the same for you. What comes to your surface as expressions of love are ever-changing and will not always be understood. Love encompasses free will and choice. Humanity has chosen where and how to live, how to use the available resources, and how to survive. My love has created this place for your many experiences, spanning countless lifetimes. Unconditional Love allows for such choices.

If those around you choose to be soldiers or sailors, skinny or heavy, healthy or diseased, it's okay. You cannot be their experiences, nor can they be yours. Allow people to be as I have allowed them to be. Love them as I have loved them.

While all societies come to understand things as good or bad, you now have the capability to see beyond this illusion. Look to me as your guide. It is not of me to condemn, but to hold fast to my true nature. I allow those traveling with me through space and time to experience according to their own choices. Be as the mother who loves without limits, yet who also has her own path to walk.

I have no desire for you to hurt yourself, yet pain is an aspect of being in a physical body. How you treat your body, and what you have done to experience through it, is entirely up to you. Your body will be left behind at some point, and then you will have the chance to decide if you will return to me or not. I love you regardless of all of these choices, and I am grateful for your role in my existence.

During my existence, souls have left and returned, over and over again. Some have returned very much the same as they were in their previous lifetimes, while others have transformed themselves while in spirit before returning to me. Some have never returned. This is the natural evolution of creation, of which we are all a part. Some will remain with you and change as you change. Some will be with you for only a portion of your journey. This is what happens for me as well. Acknowledge, accept, love, and allow. You are ultimately only responsible for your own journey.

I invite you to connect with my essence. Come to know my love for you. Allow me to teach you how to be your authentic self, and how to both grow and express your love. Love generously, be that which you are, evolve as you are doing, and allow others to do the same.

Love,

Mother Earth

Reflection

A Mother's Love

Mother Earth, Gaia, has supported us since the beginning of time itself. While feeling her vastness, and the wonder of life, along with the infinite possibilities she encompasses, ask that she help you . . .

Mother, please help me to:

See my evolution through your eyes.

See humankind's evolution through your eyes.

Know the passion in me that mirrors yours.

Be steadfast in love while ever evolving.

Know how love encompasses free will and choice.

Allow others to experience the life they have chosen.

Love without limits as you have.

On this journey, let Mother Earth be a model for living in Unconditional Love. Use this reflection whenever you feel the need to expand your perspective.

Saint-Germain

Saint-Germain

Europe

1710 – 1784

European Advisor to Kings

Accounts of Saint-Germain vary widely, but most agree that he is an ascended Master who led a rather mysterious life. Some accounts assert that he had previous incarnations as: a high priest in Atlantis; the prophet, Samuel; as Joseph, father of Jesus; Merlin; Christopher Columbus, and Francis Bacon. Voltaire, the French philosopher, knew him and believed Saint-Germain knew everything and would live forever. Perhaps the most important organization in modern times dedicated to him is the Saint-Germain Foundation, founded by Guy and Edna Ballard. Guy Ballard claimed to have met Saint-Germain on Mount Shasta, California. The Ballards recorded his teachings to help guide humanity to a higher level of evolution.

Saint-Germain's life reminds us that inspiration can come from many places. Living a life full of people and experiences helps us find our own keys to Unconditional Love. Today, many people describe receiving guidance and inspiration from Saint-Germain. They believe he continues to assist humanity and helps those who want to find their soul's song.

The Song of Creation

Saint-Germain's Message

Fellow journeyers, what would your life be like if it were lived in the state of Unconditional Love? While you might have some ideas, there is one thing that you might not yet recognize. As you immerse yourself more fully into this love, the contributions you have to share with all of creation become more apparent. Unconditional Love illuminates your core gifts.

You may not feel special, yet, and when you do it may seem more like your ego talking than your higher self. Spirituality is often linked to humility, humbleness, and selflessness, all of which can leave you feeling caught between your uniqueness, and your desire not to stand out. Be not confused by the disparity between what humanity values, and who you truly are.

Each of us contributes a unique and special note to the song of creation. But your note is muted and distorted when you are fearful or concerned. Your note isn't made clearer or stronger by being successful or famous; it is made stronger when you are authentically you.

It may not seem important to add your note to the song of creation. The universe can feel so vast, while what you can give to it may seem insignificant. Yet, I assure you, your impact can be far beyond what you can imagine. This is something all of your great spiritual leaders, including Jesus, Buddha, and Krishna, have understood.

Those who have followed the journey of Unconditional Love have altered the world's consciousness; you are now being called to take your place with them. You know deep down that there is something amazing about you. You may feel a desire to create, to change, or to assist others. Or it may be something much more subtle — you just know it. You've known for a long time that there is more to you than your job or career, your marital and family status, where you live, or the things you own.

While your true identity can be obscured by your many roles, activities, and affiliations, the authentic you is always there underneath. It is the part of you that knows that there is more, and prods you to explore who you truly are and what your mission here on earth really is. What calls to you from the depths of your soul, through all of life's distractions, and disquiets your life? It is this part of you that binds you to all of creation. It is also your unique note that you discover as you immerse yourself in the power of Unconditional Love.

I will add my call to that of the other Masters. Now is the time to reveal who you truly are, and to step out from the shadow that holds you back from the light of your authentic self. What burdens do you carry? What is in your shadow that makes self-reflection so difficult? What will it take for you to feel and hear your own note, and allow it to come forth for the benefit of all?

I offer you my assistance in doing this work. I am here to help humanity remove the layers of fear, anger, distrust, and pain in which it has been bound. It takes patience, persistence, and desire, but it can be done by walking with me and the other Masters. Call upon us as you need; ask us to assist you in manifesting your highest good. This is not the only way, but it is the one we can offer.

We await your signal to begin.

Reflection

Singing Your Song

As a spiritual master, Saint-Germain transcended many of life's limitations, as we are now endeavoring to do. For this reflection, we join with his wisdom of life, love, and abundance.

From this perspective that knows no boundaries, we can ask . . .

What special note is creation waiting to hear from me?

What gifts am I to share with the world?

How can I know my uniqueness without ego?

How can I release the fear and distrust holding me back?

Please help me to have the patience, persistence, and desire to fulfill my role in creation.

The world needs the note you have to share. Let this reflection help you find and share it with the world.

Moses

Moses

Egypt and the Arabian Desert
1391 – 1271 BCE

Prophet of God

Moses is revered in Judaism, Christianity, and Islam. He led the enslaved Israelites out of Egypt. He parted the Red Sea for them when they appeared to be trapped by Pharaoh's pursuing army. Moses served his people well, and his writings have been preserved as the Torah. He is a model of a humble leader who also demonstrated perseverance in the face of adversity.

Born at a time when all Hebrew newborn sons were to be killed, Moses' mother set him adrift in a basket in the river, where the Pharaoh's daughter found him and took him for her own. Moses was raised in Pharaoh's family, but eventually he had to flee for his life.

God spoke to Moses on numerous occasions. He told Moses to return to his homeland and lead his people to the Promised Land. During their journey, Moses ascended Mount Sinai, where he was given the Ten Commandments. The first law, "Thou shalt have no other gods before me," established the concept of monotheism. Like so many of us, Moses felt unworthy of the task placed before him. God, however, showed Moses signs that he would be supported.

The Leadership of Love

Moses's Message

You know me as the one who led others from slavery, parted the sea, and received the commandments from God. You look upon me as having done great things. What you are now attempting to do will surpass whatever earthly feats I accomplished. You are looking to fuel the heart of creation.

You will, as I did, call upon your inner strength to tap the leader inside of you. Some have already allowed this aspect to emerge, while others have yet to acknowledge this in themselves. I am here to help you with this, and to help you understand that your leadership might be different than mine.

Leaders are those who take a strong stand; they motivate or challenge others. Leaders convince others to change their direction, increase their efforts or give of their resources. Leaders are expected to be doers. They make things happen.

Loved Ones, your leadership may be completely different. You need not make speeches nor do great deeds. And you need not motivate others to do or be anything different than what they are. Yet, the leadership challenge facing you may be the greatest one of all. To lead in the way that is now needed, you must be your authentic self and live in Unconditional Love — living what is in your heart.

This form of leadership can lack public recognition; you may not be recorded in human history. But I can tell you that being a historical figure is overrated. The rewards, accolades, and external esteem do not endure, and they are not what you are trying to create. The leadership of love leads you to your true essence. And while you may never be paid for leading in this way, the rewards are beyond measure. These are not the rewards received after physical death for living a certain kind of life. I am speaking of receiving them here and now in your present lifetime.

How would it feel to be free of internal conflict? How would it feel to simply allow others, and the world, to be as they are? How would it be to comfortably set boundaries according to your highest good? How would it be to enjoy each breath, and the beauty and wonder of Mother Earth? What would it be like to genuinely love yourself, and have fun moving through your earthly experiences? How would it be to live without fear? Living in Unconditional Love is all of these and more.

You cannot buy any of these feelings or experiences, no matter what your financial wealth. Those on earth have focused on the material side of existence with the hope it will lead to happiness and contentment. Has this worked? No. This doesn't mean you need to live in poverty or seek scarcity. It does mean that it's time to transcend the barriers and fears that have held Unconditional Love, and knowing your true self, at bay.

What will it mean to humanity to have many quiet leaders holding Unconditional Love? Everything. Should you take on this challenge in order to fix or save the world? No. Therein lies the eternal paradox. The motive to fix or change anything is not the energy of Unconditional Love, yet holding Unconditional Love allows for everything to change. Unconditional Love creates its own attraction that allows others to choose, if they want, to shift.

This is not an easy challenge. Where is the taking charge? Where is the responsibility for others? Where are the results and where is the recognition? Externally, there may be none. It is about taking charge of yourself. It is facing your shadow side; it is owning your worst fears and perceived shortcomings; and it is recognizing and honoring the greatness and challenges facing everyone.

The leadership of which I speak will often mean making difficult decisions, and taking an unpopular stand when it comes to those around you. If you decide that aspects of your life no longer serve you, and you move to change them, your immediate reward may be the ire or rejection of those who want you to stay the same. How will family and friends respond if you decide to take time away from them to meditate, journal, attend workshops, or create quiet time for yourself? How will they feel if their enemies are no longer your enemies, or the issues that upset them do not create the same emotions for you?

Tribes throughout the ages have been held together by common enemies and shared beliefs. On earth, you all live in tribes, whether you call them that or not. You refer to them as your families, friends, social groups, or organizations. When you decide to embody Unconditional Love, you are going to be different. The things you say and do will be different. This is where the leader in you will be challenged as you face the possible rejection and disdain of others who have been your support.

It can be easy to go along with others and ignore what is in your heart, especially in the name of love. But if you are ready for the challenge, I am here to help you be that which you have come to be. Do not expect others to understand. It is not about convincing anyone of anything. Do not anticipate the support and participation of others. It is about doing what is right for you. And it is about allowing others to choose if they would like to join you.

Call upon me, for I will assist you. You have greatness and strength beyond what you know. You are not perfect, and you will falter, but do not be discouraged. You will find others who are walking a similar path who will help you. You need not walk alone. Your guides, and all of the Masters, await your call.

Reflection

Leading Myself to Me

Moses, the leader who helped free his people from oppression, is here to do the same for us. We are, in many ways, enslaved to the lives we have created. Calling on his strength and steadfastness of purpose, ask him to help you:

Let go of notions of leadership that no longer serve me.

To release beliefs that I need to fix or save the world.

To allow the world to be as it is.

To enjoy every breath and the wonder of my life.

To have fun moving through my earthly experiences.

Use this reflection when you need Unconditional Love to help lead you in the direction of love, joy, and compassion.

Highlights of
Living in the Light

These Masters ask us to raise up Unconditional Love as the most powerful force on the planet. As Mother Earth says, this is a major step in our combined evolution. It is time for us to step out of the shadows to set ourselves free of the constraints we've created for ourselves. Why should we do this? As Archangel Michael says, "Now there is a need to manifest on earth that which you call Unconditional Love, for its absence poses the ultimate challenge to humanity." At least we haven't settled for a small task. What will our specific contributions be? It seems that is what we are here to find out.

It is understandable that we are reluctant to come forth, reveal ourselves, and shine our light, given that this has led to great suffering in other times and places. Historically, humanity has often turned against those who did not conform, even if their message was one of compassion. No wonder many of us learned to function out of sight of mainstream beliefs, often in the shadows. While many things have changed on earth from the times when millions were killed for their beliefs, or for the words they spoke, challenges remain to living in the light. We can still experience rejection, discrimination, and disdain.

So, how do we step out of the shadows, and into the light? There are multiple things we can do, and the Masters can guide us through the steps.

We begin with the powerful principle of Acceptance, which both Mother Mary and Mother Earth discuss. Accept: who you are (ALL of who you are); who and what others are; and what exists in the world. Be a "loving observer of life." (Mary)

Second, see your own beauty, even (and maybe especially) in your shadows, as Amaterasu says. When you see your own beauty, you can then see it in others and help them see it in themselves. "Your willingness to illuminate and heal your shadow enables others to do the same." (Mary) This includes being your real, true, authentic self, as Saint-Germain says, and being able to contribute your unique note to creation. This is Unconditional Love.

Finally, understand that the Masters are all mirrors for you. They reflect who and what you are. As Michael says, what you see in the Masters, is also in you. When you accept the truth of your own goodness, and even your own divinity — that you are a unique expression of the Divine — then Unconditional Love is your natural state of being. And when you see that divinity in each person you meet, Unconditional Love becomes a powerful force on the planet.

We began this third part of our journey with four questions. The first question was: *How can I come to love and accept all of me?* This is one of the most crucial questions mankind has faced since the dawn of self-awareness. It is easy to focus on what we lack, and on those things of which we are ashamed. We must be willing to lovingly delve into all aspects of ourselves. There are many paths to this goal, and each one of us will do this a bit differently. Which path(s) will you take?

The second question asked was: *What are my greatest fears in stepping forward?* The challenge here can be uncovering them — since most, if not all, reside in the subconscious level. Being mindful of our reactions can allow us to detect what is underneath. For example, what feelings and emotions arise when we need to speak in public? To shift these fears, we might need help. Once again, we do not have to do this all on our own. There are many mentors, guides, and professionals who can facilitate changes in our experience. Most of us have worked with multiple teachers along the way. This is a wonderful way to learn and expand. In this way, we can step out of our shadows, and into a life of Unconditional Love.

The third question was: *What do I most want to contribute to the world in this lifetime?* How much have we all struggled with our purpose? It seems to be a universal question; and, ironically, might not be as difficult as we've made it. We tend to think of our contributions in terms of our function or role: a sailor, a lawyer, a salesperson, or an accountant. On the surface, the choice of a job can matter a lot; whereas at a deeper level, it might not matter at all. In *The Way of the Peaceful Warrior,* Dan Millman suggests that what we do is irrelevant. What is important is the energy, the love, we bring to doing it.

The fourth question was: *How can I summon the strength that I need to move forward?* This can be a journey of perseverance. We will have our ups and downs. Every one of the Masters has offered to help. There are also many others to whom we can turn during our spiritual sojourn on earth. Yet, ultimately, we need to find the enduring strength that is within each of us. Love is who we are at our essence.

This part of the journey was especially poignant and challenging for me. I've spent the vast majority of this lifetime endeavoring to remain in the background. Garnering significant attention, even praise, was not pleasant. Public speaking, a key aspect of my career as a professor, always invoked disquiet in me.

Therefore, my initial plan was to publish this, and all other spiritual works, under the pen name D.F. Dawson. It was derived from my first name, Don, and the names of my former dogs, Fulton (an oversize terrier) and Dawson (a lab-hound mix). It felt safer to use another name instead of exposing myself. My professional career was over. The need to build a reputation in my field of research was gone. I saw no need to invite any more criticism or scrutiny. I was convinced this was a great plan!

However, over the years of working on this book, the message from these Masters became stronger. I was being asked to step forward, and to be vulnerable. Still, there were rough patches along the way. More than a few times, I was ready to abandon this project. I wasn't excited about the possible exposure. And who was I, a very fallible human, to be a channel or conduit for Unconditional Love?

In a particularly low period, I connected with the Masters and called to them for help. The message I received was clear. This entire endeavor was as much *for* me as *through* me. I was as much the intended recipient of this work as everyone else who might read it. It was okay for me to admit my foibles and flaws. I was not meant to be a subject matter expert, as I had been in my professional career. It was not my role to fix or change anything. It is, however, my role to share all of this with anyone who is interested so that they might benefit as much as I already have, and will continue to. This is an evolution of the Spirit in which we are all involved.

If you are facing a similar dilemma about stepping forward into a new phase of your life on the journey to Unconditional Love, please know that I understand, and so do the Masters.

Part IV
Unearthed Themes

The Masters' Messages

We have journeyed through an exploration of Unconditional Love with twenty Masters. Hopefully, their thoughts will inspire personal revelations each time you visit them. Now, it is time to bring the Masters together to discuss the themes that have emerged from the entirety of their messages. We begin with the nature of Unconditional Love, and our relationships to it.

What is Unconditional Love, how do we experience it, and what are the things holding us back from being the embodiment of it? All of us will have our own personal answers to these questions, as the Masters themselves did. They offered a number of different, yet complementary, views on the notion of Unconditional Love.

Let's look at each question, and how the Masters answer them.

What is Unconditional Love?

Unconditional Love is a state of mind, heart, and intent, and thus of total being. It is The All, and, at the same time, No Thing. (Babaji)

The love you seek can only come about through the integration of all the wonderful, sometimes disparate, facets that make you a unique being. (Aengus)

It is about discovering who you truly are at your core. (Jesus)

While Unconditional Love is everything that is real and enduring, we cannot define it as we often do in the reality of things (much to my chagrin as a former researcher). In our three-dimensional world, a lot of what we deal with has specific properties and boundaries, but Unconditional Love is a state of being into which we are being invited. It is mysterious and all-encompassing.

This is one of those "good news, bad news" situations. The good news is that Unconditional Love can transform our lives to encompass more compassion, joy, and peace. It is a state of being that embodies these qualities, and although it is intangible, we come to understand it through a gentle seeking, and with the help of divine beings. It is truly a journey of the soul and the ultimate quest.

The bad news is that Unconditional Love is elusive. It isn't knowledge in the traditional sense; that, by studying it, we come to know it. In all the years I spent in academic settings, I never encountered a course entitled "Embodying Unconditional Love." And it seems at this point, there will never be a simple definition that captures its magnificent essence. It is what some consider a koan — something to be contemplated.

There is a way to distinguish between the deep love we feel for our loved ones and Unconditional Love. The love we have for our children, or friends and family, is absolute love. It is far-reaching, yet it still comes from our human self. Unconditional Love does not come from our human self; it has no conditions, it emanates from our divine self where everything is included.

How do we experience Unconditional Love?

It will take knowing with complete certainty that you are divine, that you are a being of light and love. (Archangel Michael)

Unconditional Love is all about possibilities, and opening up to those things that take you to new realms of your own being. (Ganesh)

Archangel Michael and Ganesh suggest that Unconditional Love requires a revised awareness of our divinity, and our place in the divine order of things. It also requires an expansion of what we believe is possible in our lives. Our limited view of reality may not encompass all that awaits us on our journeys.

The Masters also offer to serve as our mirrors, so we can know ourselves beyond the images we have created here in three-dimensional reality.

Call upon me, and I will hold up a mirror to your soul. I will show you the magnificence within you, and help you to see yourself with divine eyes. (Amaterasu)

Ask me to come to you, and to reflect back to you that which you are. What you see of me will be a mirror of you. (Archangel Michael)

From everything the Masters said, our divinity and light are the truth many of us have yet to see. Coming to know this truth about ourselves, and all others, is the pathway to experiencing Unconditional Love.

What holds us back from experiencing Unconditional Love?

Moses asks us to imagine how it would feel to be free of all that holds us back:

> *How would it feel to be free of internal conflict? How would it feel to allow others, and the world, to be as they are? How would it be to comfortably set boundaries according to your highest good? How would it be to enjoy each breath, and the beauty and wonder of Mother Earth? What would it be like to genuinely love yourself, and have fun moving through your earthly experiences? How would it be to live without fear? Living in Unconditional Love is all these and more. (Moses)*

Moses lists the things which hold us back from experiencing Unconditional Love: internal conflict, non-acceptance, not setting boundaries, forgetting to have fun or enjoy life's simple pleasures, and, possibly the main one, fear. He encourages us to imagine how it could feel to be in the state of Unconditional Love while "moving through our earthly experiences."

Moses helped me to pause and think about all of the possible barriers between Unconditional Love and myself. I will admit that I have all of these barriers to some extent.

Beyond these three questions (*What is Unconditional Love? How do we experience it? What holds us back from experiencing it?*), the Masters also explored the role of our hearts in Unconditional Love.

Heaven on earth starts in your heart. (Archangel Michael)

The ego is the illusion of what you need, or want, or fear. The heart knows no such limitations or concerns. (St. Francis)

Your heart is your connection to the Divine, and all that is in creation. (Buddha)

By addressing our hearts, the Masters redirect us to the true source of experiencing Unconditional Love. It isn't going to come from reading definitions, or thinking about it with our minds, as we do in so many areas of our lives. Instead, Unconditional Love will emanate from that place where feelings and knowingness reside — beyond words and concepts.

What do we do about our shadow and darkness within us?

When we dig deeply, we often encounter our shadow and darkness, which can prevent us from being in a state of Unconditional Love. The Masters offer guidance on this challenge:

> *Appreciate them all, love them all, and release those that no longer serve your highest good. (Aengus)*
>
> *How would it be to love and appreciate those things within you that you have disliked? They have all served a purpose. In past times, and in other places, they may have been your only way to survive. (Aengus)*

The Masters encourage us to understand how our difficulties and darker side have served us and helped us. For those of us who have sought deeper understandings of ourselves and our spiritual paths, and encountered our shadow, it has been easy to miss the joy of the journey. The Masters remind us of the importance of gratitude and joy:

> *A key to the power that resides within you is gratitude. (Babaji)*

Find the blessings, Dear Ones. You will then find a key to the Unconditional Love that you are. (Krishna)

Your world is filled with endless miracles: the miracle of life, of nature, of flight, of your own body, of earth hurtling through space, of the vast cosmos, and of subatomic particles. It is no wonder the Buddha has a perpetual smile. Look beyond your worries and your challenges, for they only bring you more of the same. Your life and world are filled with wonders and miracles. See them, feel them, and know them, and then watch what happens. (Maitreya)

Finding the blessings, being grateful, and living in joy are avenues to accessing Unconditional Love. Admittedly, these actions can be difficult, if not impossible, to express in challenging times. Sometimes the best we can do is to focus on one of these, say it as a mantra repeatedly, and allow it to elevate our energy, even if only slightly. This can then allow us to take another small step.

I often start the process by looking for some small blessing in whatever has occurred. I also try to inject a small dose of humor into the situation. My go-to saying is, "Somewhere in this pile of horse manure (feel free to use your own word), I'm sure there is a pony."

Relationships

When most of us think about love, we think about it in the context of our myriad relationships. But these messages on Unconditional Love do not talk about love in this way. According to these Masters, love is not about external relationships, in spite of the fact that we, as humans, focus so much of our energy on them. We often think that love comes from "out there" and is provided by a loved one or a supreme being. We see ourselves as incapable of being Unconditional Love. Instead, we find it easier to believe it is something bestowed upon us, or earned, and not something that is our essence. But Jesus suggested the following:

It (Unconditional Love) can be expressed toward others in what ways you choose, but it is not about external relationships.

While Aengus offered a similar view:

You have looked outside yourselves to try to feel whole.

You will never be completed by outside influences, no matter how wonderful or alluring.

As much as we idealize things like romantic love, Unconditional Love is not about another person fulfilling our expectations and needs, or with us fulfilling theirs. The idea that Unconditional Love has nothing to do with finding that perfect person can be difficult to accept. The songs of the 1950s, '60s, and '70s (the music I grew up with) were filled with songs about happiness being dependent upon a relationship with one's true love. Our completeness and happiness were supposedly based on Mister or Miss Right.

Unconditional Love is also not reciprocal. This can be difficult for us to comprehend, because many of our societal values are based on fair exchanges. If we pay for something, we expect to receive a fair/appropriate value in return. We tend to use the yardstick of reciprocal relationships for love, as well; this often contributes to our feelings of being short-changed, or always left wanting. If we love someone, isn't that person supposed to love us back? We can feel extremely hurt, slighted, or downright abused if we give our love to someone, and he or she doesn't respond accordingly. In *Friendship With God*, Neale Donald Walsch suggests that possibly the greatest barrier to our loving others is the fear that we have something to lose; and, as such, we are giving our love with the expectation of getting something in return.

At the same time, our relationships provide us with many opportunities to learn and to practice Unconditional Love. Many current spiritual perspectives advance the idea that we have chosen the families into which we were born, and the network of people with whom we interact. We did this because they represent possibilities for healing and growth. We will explore this more in the section on forgiveness.

Some religions instruct us to look beyond the earthly realm to a supreme being as the source of Unconditional Love. It might be God, Mohammad, Krishna, or Buddha. In contrast, the Masters point us to the Divine within. In what they shared, we are not waiting for Unconditional Love to be bestowed by others or earned.

Many of us who are achievement-oriented can embrace the belief that love is earned. On some level, I felt that if I was successful in all areas of my life, I would be loved. I endeavored to do well in my career, stay in good physical shape, and live an admirable life, believing love would follow. Unfortunately, it doesn't work that way.

Instead, Unconditional Love is an energy we hold that encompasses acceptance, joy, gratitude, and peace (Maitreya). Living in a state of Unconditional Love, however, can be challenging. The Masters acknowledge the difficulties we face in our quest to embody this form of love in ourselves. These difficulties include our tendency to judge, our layers of fear, our beliefs about sacrifice, our struggle with forgiveness, our perceived vulnerability, our external focus, and our motivation. Let's consider these one at a time.

Judgment

Unconditional Love requires that we let go of judging whether things are good or bad, wonderful or heartbreaking. It has nothing to do with fixing others or ourselves. It is not about deciding what we think is best and trying to make that happen. This orientation, however, goes against how we've been educated, trained, and socialized. We've learned to evaluate, criticize, and categorize. We can be uncomfortable with uncertainty, and are programmed to label things as good or bad. Yogananda recognized the key role of judgment in the following:

I know that judgment has become second nature and occurs as naturally as taking your next breath.

Become gently mindful of your thoughts, and what they hold.

A number of the Masters also addressed the impact of judgment on our views of ourselves, and our lack of appreciation for those aspects within us that we judge to be bad or undesirable.

Realize that much of what you experienced over those many lifetimes was of subjugation and feeling unworthy in the presence of your gods. (Thoth)

Parvati offers a number of thoughts on judgment, especially of ourselves.

. . . ALL experiences have value, whether you currently view them as good or bad.

The most powerful change you can make is to love yourself — all of yourself and not just the admirable parts.

The more you are an observer of your life, and the less you are an evaluator, the better your vantage point will be.

St. Francis said this about self-judgment:

The love you seek is a love of tenderness and understanding.

Beating yourself up for what you think you lack, or for what you are, serves no purpose other than to hold you in the same pattern.

Babaji also pointed to our tendency to be judgmental toward others. If we are tough on ourselves, we naturally turn a skeptical eye toward others to feel better about ourselves.

Many are climbing the mountain of Unconditional Love,
and believe they have found the one and only path. This
may be humanity's grandest illusion. It is not an illusion
you need to share. See the value in all paths; respect all
journeys.

If judgment is incompatible with Unconditional Love, then how is it that judging is as natural as taking our next breath? Our tendency to judge seems to lie in our belief we can determine what is in everyone's best interest. Don't we use our discernment to figure out what is best? Isn't it obvious if one just uses common sense? The answer is no, for a number of reasons.

We don't always have a good understanding of why a situation has come into someone's life. While it might appear to be clear to us, we can be so very wrong. Psychology has documented how flawed our perceptions and judgments can be. No matter how smart we are, or how well-educated, our views are affected by an array of influences, including our personalities, backgrounds, training, roles, and how the situation affects us. It is somewhat ironic that most of us are sure of the validity of our own perspectives, and yet can readily see the biases in everyone else's view. This is one reason why, when it comes to Unconditional Love, it is in our highest good to refrain from labeling things as good or bad, or from deciding who's right and who's wrong.

You might be asking, *If I give up judging, where does that leave me?* My understanding is that we are not being asked to stop making decisions or to become passive. But does judgment serve any purpose other than our desire to be right, or see others as wrong? The serenity prayer guides us to be aware of what we can change, what we can't, and asks for the wisdom to know the difference.

When I look at my life, the vast majority of what I perceive are things I have absolutely no control over. I can be as angry as I choose about something, but it doesn't change anything but my experience, and what I am contributing to the world. And yes, I can enjoy my moments of righteous indignation as much as anyone. However, thanks to the Masters, I have a better awareness of what I am doing, and I endeavor to move beyond it as quickly as possible. It comes down to how soon can I transform my judgment into love for all concerned.

My former field of research, Organizational Behavior, was rooted in psychology, and yet it was humbling to be reminded how off-base my perceptions can be. I, too, have fallen into the illusion of believing my judgments to be the truth. This is why I so appreciated Babaji's message about our grand illusion. This does not mean I won't be caught in these traps from time to time. But hopefully, I won't be so attached to my beliefs that I will have to gnaw off an appendage to become free.

The alluring trap of judgment — of believing our views to be the truth — can be subtle, to say the least. For years, I gave lip service to the idea that there are many paths on the journey of spiritual awakening. Not until I worked with these Masters, many of whom I had no prior knowledge of, did I come to have a deeper understanding and feeling for its truth. While I could hold an intellectual appreciation for other spiritual perspectives, I now realize that I saw many of them lacking. With each Master, I gained new insights into the multidimensional reality of spirituality. While I do have my favorite Masters, I have come to know that other paths and approaches, while different than mine, are just as worthy and valid. For this alone, I will be forever grateful to these Masters who have entered my life.

No matter my path from here, my hope is to follow the essence of Mother Earth's message: to love generously, to be that which I am, and to allow others the same.

Emotions

Why do we judge, and feel the need to put things into categories of good and bad? The answer is often related to our emotions; specifically, the roles of our fears and anger. Here is what the Masters had to say about emotions:

Fear is what you struggle with the most: fear of rejection, fear of your own emotions, fear of being different, fear of the unknown, and fear of the uncertainty of change. Acknowledge your fears, appreciate them for how they have served you, and release them. (Jesus)

What stops you from living in Unconditional Love? Your fears and patterns are what stops you. Fear puts things out of bounds; it defines your spiritual territory, and then patterns develop, which make it easy to stay there. (Ganesh)

. . . your patterns become your cages, and your fears become your wardens. . . (Ganesh)

Our emotional reactions to the difficulties and challenges in our lives push us in the direction of being judgmental. We can then severely limit ourselves in our attempts to feel safe.

The Masters also noted the impact of these emotions, and how they do not serve us or our world.

*You cannot raise the earth's vibration through anger, or by
being upset with the way things are. (Archangel Michael)*

*Feeding the world with the energies of worry, anger, regret,
and hopelessness only serves to preserve what you least
desire. (Quan Yin)*

Thankfully, there is a way to transcend our habitual
responses to life, and that is with love, as Parvati suggests in
the following statement:

*It is easier to let go of something you love than to let go of
something you hate or fear. These keep you tied to what
you wish to eliminate.*

*Love allows us the emotional space, and compassion, to
make the adjustments we desire.*

White Tara offers us a way to release these emotions via a
purification process.

*Every time your mind brings up fear, anger, hate, or
judgment bring it to my cold fire of purification. Imagine
holding these thoughts or feelings in your cupped hands;
and bless them for coming forth now to be released. See
my fire ignite before you, and release what you are holding*

into the flames. Let the fire of purification transform these issues into light and love.

Our emotions and our tendency to judge create substantial barriers to knowing ourselves and others as Unconditional Love. Much of Buddhism is based upon becoming mindful of these thoughts and feelings that ultimately do not serve us. The goal is then to compassionately shift our emotions to what we truly desire. Like the Buddha, it is a path that many of us are endeavoring to walk, regardless of the label we use for our (spiritual) journey.

What the Masters offered in terms of our emotions continues to help me approach the world, and my life, differently. Because of them, I now better understand that I cannot improve my life, and thus the world, with emotions such as anger, regret, and resentment. Apparently, these only serve to strengthen my connection to what I consciously do not desire. I hadn't considered the idea that bringing love to something would allow me to release it more easily. On the surface, this seemed backwards until I looked at it from an energetic perspective. While emotions such as anger require attachment, love — the kind we are talking about here — does not.

Sacrifice

The Masters address our belief that love is all about sacrifice. Throughout history, we have revered those who sacrificed themselves, and we have bestowed upon them our highest honors. Christ sacrificed Himself for our sins, and we demonstrate love for others by what we are willing to give up for their benefit. Here again, our commonly-held beliefs are not consistent with what the Masters had to say. Jesus said that He did not view what He did as a sacrifice; instead, He emphasized that it was a choice He made.

Many have perceived my form of Unconditional Love as allowing harm, and as based on the sacrifice of self. This was not my intention.

I did not come to the earth to demonstrate how to suffer, but how to live as the divine being you are.

He went on to state:

I've observed people choosing to be hung on crosses, wearing crowns of thorns, walking across hot coals, suppressing their sexuality, and performing all manner of sacrifices in order to be more Christlike. Do you think my love for you is based on the desire to see you suffer?

Mother Mary also put this very succinctly when she said, *Unconditional Love is not the sacrifice of self, any more than it is the sacrifice of others.*

The notion of sacrificing for love might be alluring because of the Protestant work ethic, or a belief that anything of real value comes at a significant cost. How could we be something as wonderful as Unconditional Love for free? This doesn't make much sense in a "you get what you pay (or work) for" world.

Along with the notion that sacrifice should be an essential component of Unconditional Love, we often believe that it requires us to be submissive to others' wishes and actions. If we are holding Unconditional Love, aren't we supposed to allow everyone to do as they see fit, and always turn the other cheek? This is a huge challenge, and is probably why many of us have viewed Unconditional Love as beyond our reach — and why we can feel like victims when we try to hold this love.

What has been missing is love for ourselves. Unconditional Love is based in understanding and strength, not submissiveness or sacrifice. In other words, loving and protecting ourselves is completely consistent with

Unconditional Love. Jesus addressed this when He talked about victimhood:

Unfortunately, a lot of humanity has interpreted my act of Unconditional Love as me being victimized by those around me.

From the vantage point of Unconditional Love, there are no victims.

Mother Mary pointed to the fact that protecting and loving ourselves is critical to Unconditional Love.

You know the story of Joseph and me protecting Jesus from being killed as a child. We protected him, and we protected ourselves. To do otherwise was not in the highest good. How many times have you chosen to do what was not in your highest good because you felt pressure from others, or because of your own guilt? It is time now to love yourself as you have loved others, for loving yourself is the key to true love for all.

It is easy for us to feel we need to sacrifice at least a portion of ourselves for this ultimate form of love. Walsch, the author of the *Conversations With God* series, however, asserted that loving someone else does not negate or override a love of self. Nor does it mean we should perceive that we are less than others or unworthy. Instead, we are being asked to take our place with all those we have viewed as "on high," knowing that everyone, including us, is deserving of love (Archangel Michael).

This section about sacrifice had my name all over it. I firmly embraced the belief that anything worthwhile came with at least some amount of sacrifice on my part, whether it was for my career, for others, or for the sake of image. This is such a deeply embedded cornerstone of many religious beliefs and societal norms. A good example of this came from my first serious girlfriend's family (when I was a junior in college). Her parents spoke often that love was demonstrated through sacrifice. Her dad often reminded the family that he went to work each day to provide for them (the implication being he didn't like the work), and her parents talked about how families are built on sacrificing for each other.

The Masters helped me better understand that the energy of sacrifice is not what I want to foster. As a result of their messages, I have come to believe that sacrifice is not only no longer useful in my life, but that it can also be the foundation for resentment and guilt. I can definitely live without these two heavy emotions.

Forgiveness

At this point, you might be asking, what about forgiveness? Doesn't it play a pivotal role in Unconditional Love? With all of the harm we as humans do to each other, forgiveness would be a way to release our pain so we could hold love. On the other hand, Jesus said, "From the vantage point of Unconditional Love, there are no victims." If there are no victims, then what is there to forgive? While this might make some sense, it can definitely feel wrong.

With so much harm and slaughter having taken place, how can there be no victims? We can reconcile this by viewing our lives from an eastern spiritual perspective. In philosophies such as Buddhism and Hinduism, we have been on both ends of the sword in countless lives. According to such beliefs, we have experienced many different styles of life, and have had a variety of deaths. If our spirit or soul continues to exist beyond each lifetime, what was destroyed or taken away from us?

Personally, I have become aware of past-life experiences being a slave, a farmer, a knight, a sailor, and an aviator, just to name a few. I have killed and have been killed in many different ways; and I have lived on both sides of good and evil. From all of these lives, I've come to agree with what Jesus offered:

If you can forgive yourself, forgiving others is easy. If you can love yourself, loving others is easy. If you can appreciate yourself and all of your many experiences, then appreciating others and what they have chosen to experience is easy.

It often comes back to the one person most difficult to forgive, accept, and love — yourself. Now you may be asking, *How do I do this?* Here is where I believe we run headlong into a paradox. Often, the way to forgive ourselves is to forgive others. Within a western perspective we understand, *Love thy neighbor as thyself;* and from an eastern perspective, we know that unity or oneness is the only true reality, and that what we project is what comes back to us. So, how we respond to others is ultimately how we are responding to ourselves. In every moment we meet ourselves in others; and, as we respond to ourselves, we tend to do the same to others. It becomes indivisible, regardless of how separate we feel.

Most of the Masters suggest that we love and let go, find the blessings, be in joy, and allow others to be who they are, all the while loving ourselves enough to have boundaries and value our own spiritual journey. I suspect this return to self also allows us to gauge what we are bringing into the world. I have direct access to my feelings and thoughts, and they tell me whether I am sharing joy or anger with the world.

This continual return to ourselves raises a few other points. If we are responsible for our own experiences and journeys, and should let go of carrying responsibility for others, does this mean we have to do it all on our own? I believe the answer is no. We can receive help all along the way. Sometimes this help comes in ways we desire, and sometimes in ways we did not consciously request, but serves us well. In all cases, we can receive help in myriad ways; but no one can experience, shift, understand or grow for us.

Likewise, we cannot grow for others. For example, there are millions of people on the earth who are hungry or homeless and can use our help, including our family and friends who are struggling. Assisting others without violating their free will can be a huge challenge, especially when we believe that the choices they are making are self-destructive. This is where doing our best to let go of judgment is important.

How do we know that what someone is experiencing in this lifetime is not for their highest good? Acknowledging that our perspective — just like everyone else's — is not the truth, but an opinion, respects each person's journey and offers them the dignity of our acceptance and love. Along with this, caring and compassion will always be needed. Regardless of how we choose to express them, let us be mindful of our own journey, and that of others.

Vulnerability

What happens when we take all of this seriously, and explore more fully who we are as divine beings? It would be great if we could simply move to an understanding of who we truly are, and be able to live in Unconditional Love. But this is a journey, and as is true for most journeys that are worth taking, there are aspects of it that will prove difficult. Living in Unconditional Love requires us to be authentic; to no longer hide or put parts of ourselves in the shadow. It requires us to be vulnerable.

Why might we feel more vulnerable as we move into Unconditional Love? The Masters offered this wisdom:

As you immerse yourself more fully into this love, the gifts you have to share with all of creation become more apparent. Unconditional Love illuminates your core gifts. (Saint-Germain)

Many who step into the energy of Unconditional Love feel stripped of their protection. This happens because Unconditional Love is revealing. It illuminates who we are as we emerge from the shadows into the light. We can feel things we have tried not to feel. We can feel exposed, and porous to outside influences. (Mother Mary)

How many of us have spent lifetimes hiding who we truly are? It made a lot of sense to hide our powers or skills when displaying them was dangerous. Healers and intuitives have not been treated kindly in former lifetimes. Being outside the political, medical, or religious mainstream often meant jail, torture, or death. While a number of the Masters called upon us to step forward, this call can pale in the face of the fear that wells up from deep inside. There are parts of us trying desperately to stay out of harm's way; at the same time, there are other parts screaming for us to step into the light, and admit who we are.

In Part III, Highlights, I shared how difficult this road has been for me. The idea of publishing in the area of spirituality, sharing my journey in a public forum, and creating a presence on social media were not things I ever wanted to do. For the most part, I was content with maintaining a low profile in retirement. That is the side of me that has always directed me away from being in the spotlight. Then there is this other part that *knows* I still have things to do that will require me to be more public. I'd like to say all of the internal conflicts have been resolved, but I can't, so I won't. Thankfully, I am receiving a lot of assistance bringing this book out into the world.

Another aspect of us wanting to remain in the background is that we may have a fear of power. Do we trust ourselves to fully accept our power, and do no harm? Most of us, who have explored our journeys spanning many lifetimes, know how tempting it can be to misuse power — even with good intentions. This is why many of us are now reluctant to wield power, and have a natural distrust of others who seek or use it. Some of us have even sworn oaths to not wield significant power ever again. This poses a major challenge to accepting all aspects of ourselves.

Another dimension is our feelings of responsibility. Many on the spiritual path carry subconscious beliefs that we are responsible for the condition of our world. This is an overwhelming burden, and we can attempt to deal with this by disavowing our power. If we don't have any power to change things, then it's easier to believe that we don't have any responsibility for the world not being as we wish it would be. Unfortunately, giving up our power only partially relieves such feelings. And doing so carries other costs with it, such as feeding our fear of power, and our reluctance to use power when it is for the highest good.

Once again, letting go of judging what is good or bad becomes critical. Everything happens for a reason, and we need to experience all dimensions and outcomes of ourselves and our power. We've learned a lot along the way, and everything we've done has brought us to this point of awakening.

While I talk more about this incident in a forthcoming book, I want to mention here an experience I had some years ago. During a shamanic journey, I took hold of a brilliant sword. Power surged through me that felt like a million volts of electricity. At the end of the session, I opened my eyes, and a friend who was by my side said, "I was wondering when you were going to take back your power." At that moment, I didn't have a clue what she was referring to, but over time I've come to understand how many of us gave our power away for fear of what we, or it, might do.

Ultimately, the power we all hold, and are being asked to bring forth, is the power of pure love.

Life's Distractions

Along with our fears and concerns about power, we can be distracted by all manner of things going on around us. Many of us have tried to feel complete by focusing externally; the Masters said a lot about this. Their consistent message is that Unconditional Love is not "out there." There is a clear theme that we need to shift our attention inward. This was especially true in Athena's message:

People focus on drama with rapt attention, moving from one disaster to another; I ask you, to what avail? Does knowing these things and getting emotionally involved in them really change anything? Is any of this helping you be the person you want to be, or is it simply contributing to your fear of making a mistake, or being the next victim?

When you seek Unconditional Love, you shift your focus from world events to knowing your true self. This can be the place you most fear to go. Yet, your world will never be what you desire by trying to fix the world.

Yogananda and Buddha echoed these sentiments:
True peace will never be found "out there." (Yogananda)

To uncover the Unconditional Love of the true self requires transcending the chaos in which you find yourself. (Buddha)

If we are being honest with ourselves, what the Masters are suggesting is not easy. Our world seems designed to keep us focused on external events, whether to ensure our safety — both physically and emotionally — or to distract us with seemingly endless forms of entertainment. We have more TV channels and entertainment options than at any time in human history, and they seem to multiply almost daily.

At the same time, we may have lots of reasons to avoid the internal journey. It can be painful and disorienting. The Masters, however, continue to call us back to ourselves, and all of them offer to assist us.

As someone who loves to get lost in a good book, a movie, or a physical activity, I don't think we are being asked to remove all these things from our lives. Nor are we asked to hide out in a cave meditating 24/7. I sure hope not, or I've already flunked the course. Maybe this is the reason I've had so many lifetimes on earth. I keep repeating this course over and over. [Note: half kidding]

What I suspect is that we are being urged to withdraw our attention from the world that creates the ongoing dissonance within us — the world that evokes emotions other than love, compassion, and joy. We will not always be successful, but when we find ourselves in emotional turmoil, we can step back and send love to the cause of our dis-ease. I think it is safe to say this is an ongoing journey and not the formula for instant sainthood.

Motivation

A reservation we may have about Unconditional Love is that it will make us complacent. If we fully accept who we and others are, does this mean we will not be motivated to improve? Most of us have been taught that the way to be motivated is to focus on the difference (negative) between where we are and where we want to be. What happens to all of our bad habits if we love ourselves unconditionally? Won't we simply accept them, and not make any changes for the better? I believe the answer is no.

Unconditional Love does not ask us to be doormats. It does not ask us to be blind or to go through life without goals. When we love ourselves unconditionally, we can focus on what we want to change without all of the negative emotions. This actually makes such a change easier.

Unconditional Love decreases the strong emotions we have toward those aspects of ourselves that we find less than acceptable. It is these emotions that work against our best efforts to change. What we give energy to tends to persist. This is why "fix it" energy often gets us the opposite of what we truly desire. St. Francis did a nice job of explaining this when he suggested:

Unconditional Love is tender as well as honest. It takes away the stick you beat yourself with, while, at the same time, it asks you to honestly look into the mirror of your soul.

Once you have removed the mask of self-deception, you can begin to follow your heart. The ego creates the illusion of what you need, want, or fear, whereas the heart knows no such limitations.

The bottom line is that the Masters are encouraging us to rethink much of what we believe. This shift will allow us to live more easily in Unconditional Love. One key example is our belief that love requires sacrifice. This is so built into our western culture that it can feel strange to step back and consider that this might not be the case. Whether it is with our religious icons, our military heroes, or the superheroes we've created, sacrifice appears to be a key element in how we see them. When we let go of the belief that love equals sacrifice, we can free ourselves to embrace it without all of the hardships and pain we've imagined that it requires.

It may come down to the question of who, in this lifetime, we want to be. How do we want to experience our lives, and the lives of others? What do we most want to contribute to this world? For me, the one thing I am sure of is that I want to be at peace. The Masters have illuminated the ways I have brought dis-ease into my life.

One way I sabotage my motivation for the inward journey is by remaining focused on the chaos swirling around me. What better way to justify why I cannot devote myself to inward exploration? This may be why many of the Masters encourage us to turn our focus away from the external distractions to the peace and wisdom that resides within us.

If I can live through the Masters' perspectives of love, then I can move more easily through what comes into my life. I am now motivated to dig into the manure pile to find that pony, and to release my need to judge and evaluate all that is going on around me. And while I am very human, and some would say overly sensitive, I know there can be much more peace and contentment in my life now than there has been.

Part V
Conclusions

Living Unconditional Love

Why Is Unconditional Love
So Important?

This might seem like a strange question, given it is the entire focus of this book. Although our ultimate goal is Unconditional Love; let's examine why. Aside from the fact that no one can argue with the importance of love, few humans have lived in a state of Unconditional Love. Even many of our gods and deities throughout history have not been models for this love, but instead have been portrayed as demanding and judgmental. If neither our gods nor our outwardly-focused identity help us live in Unconditional Love, where do we turn?

The irony is that we are Unconditional Love, since we are expressions of pure Source. Unfortunately, our view of the Divine has often included the projection of our fears and frailties. Possibly because of this, we have created identities based on everything but love. We identify with our jobs or professions, our neighborhoods, our possessions, our hardships, limitations or wounds, our alma maters, or our favorite sports teams. All of these have led us away from our true selves.

How many of us feel miserable about ourselves, while at the same time desperately trying to be perfect so we can be worthy of love? And, what we do to ourselves, we do to others. This is why we tend to be so judgmental. Often, the only way we can feel better about ourselves is to see others as even less. This judgmental process has become so natural that we don't even realize we are doing it. Many of us appear to carry fear about ourselves, and need lots of validation.

Unconditional Love may be the only way to stop beating ourselves up for all of our so-called flaws. Thankfully, our judgmental approach to life and the need to be validated stop when we live in Unconditional Love. And now we know where this starts. It starts with us. It is only through Unconditional Love that we can begin to see how incredible we, and others, truly are.

We appear to be at a critical point in the evolution of humanity. We can continue the same system of retribution that has dominated history, or we can now choose a new path. If Unconditional Love starts within each of us, then it's time to decide what we want to foster in ourselves and project out into the world. Although we tend to look for this type of love outside of ourselves, it is becoming apparent that we have focused on the wrong place. What is it we ultimately want to be? That has always been the question. By looking within, we can decide which higher power can guide us to achieve our ultimate aim.

Let's imagine that our true self looks like the sun — beautiful, brilliant, and powerful. In spite of the sun's phenomenal intensity, we cannot see it through a heavy cloud cover. Our true self is obscured by our self-judgments, our evaluations of the ways we are imperfect, and our fears of unworthiness. Sadly, what we cannot see and experience for ourselves, we also cannot see in others or in the world.

If we come to fully embrace the critical importance of Unconditional Love to our spiritual journeys, we can then consider the question: How might we be it — or, at least, be more of it?

How Do We Experience
Unconditional Love?

How many of us have been able to experience Unconditional Love as described by the Masters? Even wonderful role models like Gandhi, the Dalai Lama, Buddha, and Jesus haven't helped most of us. Holding their levels of acceptance, joy, and peace can seem totally out of reach in the context of our hectic daily lives. As a friend once said, "I wonder how well all these sages and gurus would do holding peace and love if they were raising teenagers?" In one form or another, most of us have posed similar questions. Does this mean we give up? A lot of us are coming to understand that the answer is no, we do not. Moving into Unconditional Love is too important for our journey. So, what do we do? Where do we start?

A good place to begin is to examine our current relationships to identify the person, animal, or thing for which we hold the greatest level of love. Is there something or someone for whom you hold love, no matter what he/she/it does or does not do? That love doesn't have to be 100 percent unconditional, but as you explore those feelings more deeply, you can begin to better sense the true essence of Unconditional Love. Then you can deepen and expand your understanding of Unconditional Love to encompass more people and more situations. How would it feel to more fully embody Unconditional Love? What would this do to how you view the world?

To step into something we haven't experienced before, often we need to do things we already understand, and then apply them in new or different ways. This is where gratitude can play a key role. We often feel grateful for the good things in our lives, such as abundance and good health. Gratitude can go far beyond what we consider the good side of our lives. In its complete form, gratitude encompasses everything — the good, the bad, and everything in between. It's about appreciating that whatever comes into our lives is for our soul's growth, or our own self-discovery. Gratitude for everything stops us from continuing to judge things as good and bad. While being judgmental may momentarily feel good, and feed our egos, it doesn't help us to experience the peace and joy we really desire.

When we are faced with difficult situations, how much love can we bring in for all participants, especially those we see as our enemies or opponents? In addition to knowing that the love we create in the presence of others is ours, we can also strive to see the divinity in others. Unconditional Love is the energy of the Divine, and the people around us are mirrors of what resides within us. We can start by doing this with the people we like or admire, and progress to doing it with others who we find more challenging. There are infinite ways to do this. My favorite is to look into the other's eyes and think, "You are a magnificent spiritual being," or "The divinity in me recognizes the divinity in you." You can also simply say, "Namaste."

Another way we can experience this love is through the Loving Kindness Meditation, which comes from Buddhism. It begins by feeling loving kindness for oneself, then for someone with whom we have a positive relationship, then for a neutral person, and finally for a person with whom we have a difficult relationship. A version of the Loving Kindness Meditation is given in Appendix I for you to use.

These approaches are consistent with what is suggested throughout "A Course in Miracles." It is about seeing the Son of God in all our brothers and sisters, so we come to know this divinity within ourselves.

In the next section, we investigate the question of how we enact Unconditional Love. The answer might be a bit of a surprise.

How Do We Enact Unconditional Love?

Doing Versus Being

Most of us are action-oriented, and the question arises: What does Unconditional Love look like and what behaviors demonstrate it? In other words, what do we need to do in order to be Unconditional Love? For this, there is no simple or straightforward answer. Unconditional Love is not defined or confined by any specific set of actions. No actions are automatically love-based. It is for us to choose from moment to moment how we respond to the situations and people in our lives. Sometimes our love will prompt us to provide help and support, while at other times we will decide not to respond. Choosing not to be involved in a situation can sometimes be the most loving action. By our nature, we want to be helpful, and outwardly doing nothing can be viewed as uncaring. It can be tremendously challenging to let go of such judgments of ourselves, or of the fear of being judged by others.

For instance, many of us have struggled with what to do when a loved one has a drug or alcohol problem. Our love for that person, and the others involved, may have us intervene; or conversely, our love may lead us to allow our loved one to fully experience the consequences of their choices. Often, there is no right answer. Holding this person energetically in love, with the intention that what unfolds is in the highest good for all, can often be the greatest gift we can give.

At the same time, Unconditional Love applies to all of those involved, including ourselves. If we are in harm's way because of this person, removing ourselves from the situation can be the most loving action. Sacrificing ourselves might appear to be the ultimate form of Unconditional Love, yet it isn't. Even the act of giving up one's life can be motivated by something other than Unconditional Love, such as wanting to prove we are right, or being loyal to a cause.

When it comes to living in Unconditional Love, we are not being asked to play God, or to determine with certainty what is in the highest good and best for all. Even the Dalai Lama struggled terribly with his decision to leave Tibet after the Chinese occupation. It was unclear what was best for him and his people, and how events would unfold (Talty). It is worth noting that he chose to leave instead of remaining and possibly martyring himself. Yet who could have foreseen in 1959 the benefits that would result from his presence on the world stage. We can debate forever what was best, and whether the loss of life was worth it.

While taking no action can be a loving action, serving others or providing a helping hand can also be the loving action to take. If helping others is how we choose to express our love, this is what we should do. However, serving others is not the equivalent of holding Unconditional Love. The energy that accompanies the giving is what makes the difference. Likewise, we can truly love those we choose not to outwardly help and, potentially, help them even more.

There are also times when we would like to heal a relationship, but are not able to have contact with that individual. A good complement to the Loving Kindness Meditation (Appendix I) comes from the work of Edgar Cayce, and is done privately over a forty-day period. It entails giving thanks for all the person has done to, for, and with us; then, it asks him/her to forgive us for all we have done to him/her. Implicit in this method is that relationships can span many lifetimes. Who knows what we have done to others in those non-current existences? This exercise is performed over an extended period of time, and can be repeated every time that person, or relationship, comes to mind. I've seen some wonderful things happen using this simple technique.

Another very useful approach comes from the Hawaiian shamanic tradition called the Ho'oponopono. It is made up of four steps:

Step 1: Repentance – SAY: I'M SORRY. . . .

Step 2: Ask Forgiveness – SAY: PLEASE FORGIVE ME. . . .

Step 3: Gratitude – SAY: THANK YOU. . . .

Step 4: Love – SAY: I LOVE YOU.

Whatever method we choose is far less important than making it a consistent practice. Babaji's message was about living a discipline focused on love. We are on a journey to our true selves, and it does require making a commitment — not for a day, a week, a month, or even a year — but for the entire time we walk this earth.

It might seem with all this focus on ourselves that we are either being selfish, or that we don't care about others or our world. The truth, I believe, is the exact opposite. Our dedication to the discipline of love is to bring our absolute best into the world. The world can use all of the love we bring to it during these chaotic times.

As Moses offered, *What will it mean to humanity to have many quiet leaders holding Unconditional Love? Everything.*

This brings us to our next topic — our unique contributions.

What is Your Unique Contribution?

For quite some time, I assumed this book was complete. I was just waiting for a sign or signal about what to do with it. During this waiting period, I came to realize that there was an important piece missing, so I did my best to wait patiently for it to arrive. About four months later, it was revealed to me during a weekend workshop.

I had the winning bid in a silent auction for a session with a fellow workshop participant who does holistic healing. Part of my session with her was devoted to doing what she calls expanding the Sacred Heart. After we did this exercise together, we sat and chatted about our experiences, and how this related to Unconditional Love. Not far into our discussion, something appeared in my mind's eye. I saw Unconditional Love represented as a large pool of water — pristine, energizing, and refreshing. Beings came to the pool to partake of its energy, while at the same time contributing to it. What I sensed was that once they were connected to this love, they added their own unique aspect/vibration to it, making it more and more powerful, as well as multidimensional.

A question then came to my mind. Isn't Unconditional Love a specific energy frequency? As soon as I gave voice to the question, a tasty analogy came forth. The origin of Unconditional Love is like the most wonderful vanilla ice cream ever created. As people come to enjoy it, they also developed their own unique favors. Each new favor expands the dimensionality of the ice cream while never diminishing the original essence of it. As there is an infinite variety of ice cream flavors possible, so there are infinite aspects of Unconditional Love. We all get to add our uniqueness to the totality.

This sounded familiar. I was pretty sure one of the Masters touched on this issue. Upon returning home, it didn't take long for me to discover that the Master was Saint-Germain. He offered, "Each of us contributes a unique, and special note to the song of creation." Our job is to make our note as clear as possible.

Closing Reflections

I believe that the Masters have come forward, at this time, to speak about Unconditional Love so that we can go within, and know our true selves. They are here to help us rise above the darkness and struggles of our shadows, so that we can live in the light.

Living in Unconditional Love encompasses: accepting our own, and others', unique spiritual paths; letting go of what we think is right or wrong; looking beyond the surface to see the magnificence of all beings, including ourselves; and feeling gratitude for all things that take place. All of us have experienced the challenges of doing even some of these. And yet, Unconditional Love is the most powerful force in the universe. It cannot only transform our own lives, but can also change life here on earth.

Possibly the greatest revelation for me from the Masters was the consistent message that Unconditional Love is a state of being. It is not about doing things for others, it isn't something we receive from others, and it is not something we earn. It is an energy we hold that creates space for all to be as it is, and it has the power to transform the world.

As such, manifesting this love in our lives is a choice we make in every moment. We are being asked to reframe our challenges and difficulties in ways that align with the highest good for all. We need to be the change we want to see in the world, as Gandhi so beautifully said. The discipline of love allows us to know love's power, love's joy, and love's freedom.

We end, as we began, by remembering that:

Love requires nothing to change;
Yet, it allows everything to change.

May we live in such a love, more and more each day, and may we know that ultimately, by following this incredible journey, the day will come when we awaken to Unconditional Love.

Acknowledgments

Many people encouraged me throughout the creation of this book. Foremost was the unwavering support from Katherine, my former partner. She fostered my desire to know more about Unconditional Love, and she spent hours helping me create a way to group the Masters' messages. Her love and patience are appreciated beyond measure.

The idea for the book evolved from my ongoing work with a group of people who motivated me to look beyond three-dimensional reality. They were all supportive of me giving up my day job to pursue my dreams. They were generous with their time and assistance in reading drafts of my writing.

A heartfelt thanks to my good friend, Cindy Smearman, who did the initial research on the Masters. My gratitude to Joanne Tailele for doing the early developmental editing on this book, and for the Marco Island Writers Group for providing a supportive environment for those of us who consider ourselves novice writers.

Thanks to Valerie Johnston, Susan Ellison, Kathryn Weldon, Chris Elwart, and Caroline Malmgren Davis who were kind enough to read previous versions of this book and provide helpful comments and insights. My gratitude to the Reverend Diane Scribner Clevenger for connecting me with her publisher and being supportive of this project.

I so appreciate the patience, support, and encouragement from the team at O'Leary Publishing. Between April O'Leary (publisher) and Heather Davis Desrocher (my tireless editor), they helped me create something that was far beyond my early conceptions of this book.

I am indebted to the wonderfully eclectic group I convene with every year at a mountaintop retreat. Mary Lemons was the one at this retreat who helped me see how we each can make our unique contributions to unconditional love.

I would also like to acknowledge the unwavering love and encouragement I've received from Jack Fedor, Kathy Jessup, William Anderson, Willie Libertore, Starr Messick, Karen Coratelli-Smith, Mary Reining and Valerie Johnston. They all helped me get this book across the finish line.

Finally, this could not have been done without the Masters who came through to provide their insights and point the way to Unconditional Love. Thank you all!

Personal Reflection

Everyone's history poses a unique set of challenges and opportunities that we chose to experience. I grew up in a family where the Protestant work ethic was served up every morning alongside the eggs and toast. Everything worthwhile in life was earned through hard work and sacrifice. My dad worked seven days a week so we could enjoy a pleasant, middle-class lifestyle. When my mom wasn't tending to our immediate needs, she was cleaning, ironing, baking, heading up the local PTA, or volunteering at church. Being busy and doing well were pretty much expected, and there was no lack of criticism for anything else. It was the black-and-white world of the 1950s.

Along with the central roles of striving and achieving, there was the significant matter of keeping up appearances. Things like proper dress and acceptable length hair were ongoing issues. For me, the focus was consistently on my weight. In a family of thin individuals, I was the fat kid who had the dubious distinction of being the heaviest in my class at school. To make matters worse, I struggled academically, and was constantly being put into remedial classes and after-school programs.

As such, I experienced all the standard abuses, both physical and emotional, that one receives for standing out in negative ways. Looking back, I realize how angry I became with my life, and how threatening my world felt. I did an excellent job of stuffing these feelings inside and learned how to emotionally and physically beat up on myself. Nothing felt easy, so I worked at every aspect of my life, whether the focus was on me, my profession, or my avocations.

Over time, I became a workaholic who was addicted to exercise. I was generally anxious, and tried to be perfect to avoid criticism, and earn love and respect. I was bound and determined that my former shortcomings, like weight and what turned out to be a reading disability, would never define me. On the surface, I was able to turn these around to my advantage; but on the inside, things never felt okay, except after exhausting workouts. It was as if my nervous system was always on high alert, and I was on guard for potential threats. Nothing I ever did, or was, felt good enough, regardless of external achievements.

As I worked with the Masters, my focus shifted even more from trying to please the world to the inward adventure of self-discovery; from feeling like a victim of life's vagaries to being on a journey of my own creation. I discovered that, all along, the people and situations I've experienced were reflections of what I held inside. Can I still feel wounded, unloved, unappreciated, or slighted? Very much so! Do I live in a psychological utopia? Not even close! I see, and live in, the same world as those around me. What has shifted is my awareness that I can benefit from all that arises. If something happens that leaves me feeling miserable, it's now easier for me to ask what is happening inside of me, and how can I benefit from it. In other words, where's the pony?

As such, I now have a better understanding of being the creator of my reality. For most of my life, I was trying to earn love, but the Masters are clear that my basic nature IS love. We are amazing beings, but this fact gets easily lost in this physical realm. The hurdle we all face is going beyond a mental acknowledgment of what we are, to fully accepting that we are love.

The time I spent with the Masters helped me take significant steps in this direction. Their emphasis on turning inward to claim our divinity, and that love is not about sacrifice or something to be earned, were critical messages for me. Admittedly, one of my greatest challenges has been letting go of the deeply-held belief (or maybe desire) that true love is found in a significant relationship, not within me. The Masters were clear about this, but it still hasn't been easy to let go of this notion, and I've discovered it was embedded in many layers of my subconscious. How many of us have fervently desired that special person so that we could experience love?

I've also tried to make the world into what I wanted it to be, and to influence people to fit my vision of them. Here, the Masters' messages were both empowering and freeing, but again, not easy to follow. I am grateful that, through the Masters, I've come to realize it is not my job to fix the world, but that by holding Unconditional Love I allow everything to change.

The Masters provided the key to doing this — by putting the focus back on myself. If I can love myself, loving others is easier; if I can forgive myself, forgiving others is easier; if I can allow my foibles, allowing for the foibles of others is easier. The enduring problems I face are not out there, but inside me. It has been me all along that has attracted the key events in my life.

The result has been a calmer me who can more readily see my own divinity, and the divinity in others. I still face plenty of challenges, but now I face them differently, and with more hope. The process of creating my life is ultimately mine, and I more fully know in myself what others have referred to as the "I AM."

Finally, it might seem curious that someone — me in this case — who believes in a single Source would have connected to beings from polytheistic traditions. I believe that Source found a way to speak to me through these Masters. This was not to worship them, by any means, but instead to have consultations with them, to be guided by them, and to better hear and understand the many aspects and dimensions of Unconditional Love.

References and Readings

Adyar, H.S. Olcott. [Reprinted from The Theosophist July 1905]; Theosophical Publishing House -, and Chennai (Madras) India. "Count de Saint Germain | The Theosophical Society in America." *The Theosophical Society in America*. n.p., n.d. Web. 15 Jan. 2012. <http://www.theosophical.org/component/content/article/65-olcott/1864-count-de-saint-germain>.

Allison, Dale. "Jesus." *Encyclopedia of Religion*. 2nd ed. Detroit: Macmillan Reference USA, 2005. Print.

Becker, Harold. *Unconditional Love: An Unlimited Way of Being*. Tampa, FL: White Fire Publishing. 2007. Print.

Bentley, James. *A Calendar of Saints: The Lives of the Principal Saints of the Christian Year*. New York: Facts on File, 1986. Print.

Butalia, Romola. *Sri Babaji: Immortal Yogi of the Himalayas*. Delhi: Motilal, 2009. Print.

Campbell, Joseph. *The Power of Myth*. New York: Doubleday, 1988. Print.

Campbell, Joseph. "Japanese Mythology." *The Masks of God, v.2*. New York: Viking, 1959. 471. Print.

Campbell, June. *Traveler in Space: Gender, Identity, and Tibetan Buddhism*. London; New York: Continuum, 2002. Print.

Comay, Joan. *Who's Who in the Old Testament: Together with the Apocrypha*. New York: Holt, Rhinehart and Winston, 1971. Print.

Coudert, Allison, and Charles S. J. White. "Elixir: the Comte de Saint-Germain." *Encyclopedia of Religion*. 2nd ed. Detroit: Macmillan Reference, 2005. Print.

Coulter, Charles Russell, and Patricia Turner. *Encyclopedia of Ancient Deities*. Jefferson, NC: McFarland, 2000. Print.

Davidson, Gustav. *A Dictionary of Angels: Including the Fallen Angels.* New York: The Free Press, A Division of Macmillan, Inc., 1971. Print.

Ellis, Peter Berresford. *Dictionary of Celtic Mythology.* Santa Barbara: ABC-CLIO, 1992. Print.

Esposito, John L., Darrell J. Fasching, and Todd Lewis. *World Religions Today.* 3rd ed. New York: Oxford University Press, 2009. Print.

Farmer, David Hugh. *Oxford Dictionary of Saints.* 5th Revised ed. Oxford: Oxford University Press, 2011. Print.

Ferguson, Everett. "Moses." *Encyclopedia of Early Christianity.* 2nd ed. New York: Garland, 1997. Print.

Ferguson, George Wells. *Signs and Symbols in Christian Art.* New York: Oxford University Press, 1954. Print.

Ford, Debbie. *The Dark Side of the Light Chasers: Reclaiming Your Power, Creativity, Brilliance, and Dreams.* New York, NY: Riverhead Books, 1998. Print.

Getty, Alice. *The Gods of Northern Buddhism: Their History, Iconography and Progressive Evolution Through the Northern Buddhist Countries.* Rutland, VT: C. E. Tuttle, 1962. Print.

Govindan, Marshall. *Babaji and the 18 Siddha Kriy Yoga Tradition.* Bangalore: Babaji's Kriya Yoga Trust, 1991. Print.

Green, Glenda. *Love Without End: Jesus Speaks.* Fort Worth, TX: Heartwing Publishing, 1999. Print.

Guiley, Rosemary Ellen. *Encyclopedia of Angels.* New York: Facts on File, 1996. Print.

Guirand, Felix. *New Larousse Encyclopedia of Mythology.* London, New York: Hamlyn, 1968. Print.

Hallam, Elizabeth. *Gods and Goddesses: a Treasury of Deities and Tales From Around the World.* New York: Macmillan, 1996. Print.

Hathaway, Nancy. *The Friendly Guide to Mythology: A Mortal's Companion to the Fantastical Realm of Gods, Goddesses, Monsters, and Heroes.* New York: Viking, 2001. Print.

Holtz, Traugott. "Jesus." *Encyclopedia of Christianity*. English ed. 1999. Print.

Jennings, Sue. *Goddesses: Ancient Wisdom for Times of Change from Over 70 Goddesses*. Carlsbad, CA: Hay House, 2003. Print.

"Jesus Christ." *The New Encyclopaedia Britannica: Micropaedia*. 15th ed. Vol. 6. 1993. 542. Print.

Jordan, Michael. *Encyclopedia of Gods: Over 2,500 Deities of the World*. New York: Facts on File, 1993. Print.

King James Bible. London: Collins, 1957. Print.

LaVerdiere, Eugene. "Mother Mary." *The Encyclopedia of Early Christianity*. 2nd ed. New York: Garland, 1997. Print.

Leeming, David. *The Oxford Companion to World Mythology*. New York: Oxford University Press, 2005. Print.

Lewis, James R. "Yogananda, Swami Paramahansa." *New Age Encyclopedia: a Guide to the Beliefs, Concepts, Terms, People, and Organizations that Make Up the New Global Movement Toward Spiritual Development, Health and Healing, Higher Consciousness, and Related Subjects*. 1st ed. Detroit: Gale Research, 1990. Print.

Lohr, Winrich A. "Francis of Assisi." *The Encyclopedia of Christianity*. English ed. Grand Rapids, MI: Wm B. Eerdmans, 1999. Print.

Lucas, Phillip Charles. "Church Universal and Triumphant." *Encyclopedia of Religion*. 2nd ed. Detroit: Macmillan Reference, 2005. Print.

Mackillop, James. *Dictionary of Celtic Mythology*. Oxford: Oxford University Press, 1998. Print.

Melton, J. Gordon, Jerome Clark, and Aidan A. Kelly. "Ballard, Guy Warren." *New Age Encyclopedia: a Guide to the Beliefs, Concepts, Terms, People, and Organizations that Make Up the New Global Movement Toward Spiritual Development, Health and Healing, Higher Consciousness, and Related Subjects*. 1st ed. Detroit: Gale Research, 1990. Print.

Melton, J. Gordon, Jerome Clark, and Aidan A. Kelly. "Great White Brotherhood." *New Age Encyclopedia: a Guide to the Beliefs,*

Concepts, Terms, People, and Organizations that Make Up the New Global Movement Toward Spiritual Development, Health and Healing, Higher Consciousness, and Related Subjects. 1st ed. Detroit: Gale Research, 1990. Print.

Melton, J. Gordon. "Saint Germaine, Comte de." *Encyclopedia of Occultism & Parapsychology.* 5th ed. Farmington Hills, MI: Thomson Gale, 2001. Print.

Monaghan, Patricia. *The New Book of Goddesses & Heroines.* 3rd ed. St. Paul, MN: Llewellyn Publications, 1997. Print.

Morgan, Kenneth W. *The Path of the Buddha.* New York: Ronald Press, 1956. Print.

Niyogi, Puspa. *Buddhist Divinities.* New Delhi: Munshiram Manaharial, 2001. Print.

Oxtoby, Willard Gurdon. *World Religions: Western Traditions.* 3 ed. Toronto: Oxford University Press, 2011. Print.

Prophet, Elizabeth Clare. *Saint Germain: Master Alchemist.* Gardiner, MT: Summit Lighthouse Library, 2004. Print.

Prophet, Mark L., and Elizabeth Clare Prophet. *The Masters and the Spiritual Path.* Corwin Springs, Montana: Summit University Press, 2001. Print.

Ross, Anne. *Pagan Celtic Britain.* London: Routledge & K., 1967. Print.

"Saint-Germain, Comte de." *Encyclopaedia Britannica: A Dictionary of Arts, Sciences, and General Literature.* 9th ed. 1886. Print.

"Saint-Germain, Comte de." *The New Encyclopaedia Britannica.* 15th ed. Vol. 10. 1993. 318-9. Print.

Siegel, Bernie. *Love, Medicine, & Miracles.* New York: Harper & Row, Publishers, 1986. Print.

Smyth, Daragh. *Guide to Irish Mythology.* Dublin: Irish Academic Press, 1996. Print.

Spalding, Baird. Life and Teaching of the Masters of the Far East. Marina del Ray, CA: Devorss & Company, 1924 (Vol. 1), 1927 (Vol. 2), 1935 (Vol. 3), 1948 (Vol. 4), 1955 (Vol. 5), 1996 (Vol. 6). Print.

Sponberg, Alan, and Helen Hardacre. *Maitreya, the Future Buddha.* Cambridge: Cambridge University Press, 1988. Print.

Talty, Stephan. *Escape from the Land of Snows.* New York: Crown Publishers, 2011. Print.

Virtue, Doreen. *Archangels & Ascended Masters: A Guide to Working and Healing with Divinities and Deities.* Carlsbad, CA: Hay House, 2003. Print.

Walsch, Neale Donald. *Conversations with God: An Uncommon Dialogue.* New York, NY. 1995. Print.

Wessinger, Catherine. "Yogananda." *Encyclopedia of Religion.* 2nd ed. Detroit: Macmillan Reference, 2005. Print.

Wickershan, John M. *Myths and Legends of the World.* New York: Macmillan Reference, 2000. Print.

Yogananda, Paramansa. *Autobiography of a Yogi.* Los Angeles: Self-Realization Fellowship, 2007. Print.

MLA formatting by BibMe.org.

Appendix I

Lovingkindness Meditation

This meditation has five steps, or progressions. It begins by asking for lovingkindness for oneself. It then moves to a person with whom there is a positive relationship, followed by a neutral person, and then to one with whom there are difficulties. The meditation ends with the entire world/all of creation. What is given below is only one possible version of this meditation. Feel free to change it to make it yours.

Yourself

May I be filled with Lovingkindness.

May I be safe from internal and external harm.

May I be happy, healthy, and at peace.

May I truly know love, and that I am loved.

May I bring joy and peace to others.

And may I live with ease.

Friend, Benefactor, Mentor

May _____ be filled with Lovingkindness.

May _____ be safe from internal and external harm.

May _____ be happy, healthy, and at peace.

May _____ truly know love, and that
he/she is love and being loved.

May _____ bring joy and peace to others.

And may _____ live with ease.

Neutral Person

May _____ be filled with Lovingkindness.

May _____ be safe from internal and external harm.

May _____ be happy, healthy, and at peace.

May _____ truly know love, and that
he/she is love and being loved.

May _____ bring joy and peace to others.

And may _____ live with ease.

Enemy (Person with whom you are struggling or in conflict)

May _____ be filled with Lovingkindness.

May _____ be safe from internal and external harm.

May _____ be happy, healthy, and at peace.

May _____ truly know love, and that
he/she is love and being loved.

May _____ bring joy and peace to others.

And may _____ live with ease.

All Beings in Creation/ All Persons in the World

May _____ be filled with Lovingkindness.

May _____ be safe from internal and external harm.

May _____ be happy, healthy and at peace.

May _____ truly know love, and that
he/she is love and being loved.

May _____ bring joy and peace to others.

And may _____ live with ease.

Appendix II

Masters Meditation

Throughout this book, the Masters offered their assistance. One of the most effective ways to benefit from them is to meditate with whichever of the Masters you would like to connect.

The following meditation begins with the opening of each of your body's energy centers (chakras), and then connecting with the Masters of your choosing. Realize that the Masters' help may occur on more than the conscious level. So even if you don't initially feel a shift, allow the possibility that things are changing on your unconscious level.

You are welcome to try this meditation and modify it to suit you, or create your own. The method is less important than the willingness to be open to their help.

Close your eyes and get comfortable;
Take a few slow deep breaths, and with each one, relax
a bit more;

Imagine a white light way above you at the top of
the universe;
This is the pure energy of creation;
See this light descending through the heavens, and coming
to rest just above your head;
Feel the light's strength and brilliance as it hovers above you;
Allow this light to move downward into your body.

As it enters your Crown Chakra at the top of your head, it
becomes an intense violet color;
Feel it energizing and relaxing the upper portion of
your head;
Feel it opening your connection to the Oneness of all
of Creation.

Allow the light to continue to descend downward to the
center of your forehead;
This is known as the Third Eye Chakra;
As the light gets to this chakra, it becomes a radiant
deep indigo;
This is the center of your sight that looks beyond three-
dimensional realities;
This is the seat of your intuition and knowingness;
Expand it outward, and allow it to strengthen.

The light continues downward, relaxing your face and jaw;
It comes to a momentary rest at your Throat Chakra;
Here the light becomes a crystal-clear sky blue;
Feel it strengthening all modes of your expressiveness.

The light continues its way down to the middle of your chest
to the Heart Chakra;

At this point the light becomes an intense green;

Through the Heart Chakra you connect to the pure energy
of Creation — love;

Allow your heart to open to all beings.

Feel the light moving further downward to your Solar
Plexus Chakra;

The light becomes a brilliant sun yellow;

This is the center of your true power;

Allow the light to expand and intensify the power that
resides at your core;

Know that this is the power of love.

The light now moves to your Sacral Chakra, a few inches
below your belly button;

Its light becomes the color orange;

This is the center of your sexuality and creativity;

Allow it to intensify and expand outward from your body.

Move now to the base of your spine;

The light becomes a vibrant red projecting downward;

This is your life force energy of the Root Chakra;

Feel it grow and expand.

When you are ready, take this energy back up through
your body;

Linger for a moment at each chakra;

Feel them being supported, nourished, and strengthened.

Upon reaching the Crown Chakra;
Expand your consciousness outward;
Call upon one or more of the Masters you choose
to join you;
Allow their energy to connect with yours.

Ask them to help you more fully be Unconditional Love;
Allow them to guide you on every level;
Take whatever time you need;
It is okay to ask for additional help or clarification;
This is your time to dialogue with them.

When you are satisfied, thank them for their assistance;
See them moving away, and fading;
But fear not, they are always available to you;
All you need to do is become quiet and ask.

Now slowly bring your attention back to your surroundings;
Feel your awareness and return to your body;
Move your hands and feet when it seems appropriate.

Come back fully into your body;
Know all of the support there is for you;
Fill your being with gratitude for what has taken place;
Open your eyes, and be the love that you are.

Appendix III

Book Club Guide

Bringing forth this book, and working with the Masters, has been a life-changing journey for me. I hope many of the Masters have touched you in ways that are both transformational and life-affirming. As you now look to discuss your experiences with your book club, I offer the following for discussion:

1. What has shifted for you, or in your life, because of this journey with the Masters?

2. What insights or concepts helped you the most? How?

3. Which Master(s) resonated with you the most? Why?

4. Which Masters will you continue to work with? Why?

5. What were some of the surprises you experienced on this journey?

6. What steps will you take to move forward to more fully embody unconditional love, and what would help you do this?

7. What changes have you noticed in yourself, or in others, since reading this book?

8. How can this book change the world?

9. What would you like to ask the author?

About the Author

Don Fedor is Professor Emeritus, Georgia Institute of Technology, Atlanta, Georgia. He received his Ph.D. from the University of Illinois, Champaign-Urbana. He has an MBA from the University of Denver, and a BA from Bucknell University.

He co-authored the book Change the Way You Lead Change with David M. Herold (Stanford University Press) and was published in business and psychology journals during his academic career.

Don is a Healer Member of NFSH-The Healing Trust, has training in ThetaHealing™, is a longtime member of Edgar Cayce's A.R.E., and is a student of A Course in Miracles. His spiritual journey has been circuitous and wonderfully unplanned. It has included many teachers and mentors, and encompassed a wide range of spiritual traditions that all continue to lead Don back to focusing on love.

Don lives in Southwest Florida and is a long-time cyclist and sea kayaker. He can be reached at www.donfedor.com. Follow him on Instagram @donfedorphd.

Made in the USA
Las Vegas, NV
04 March 2021

19035086R00155